Manage Your Time/
Market Your Business

Manage Your Time/ Market Your Business

The Time-Marketing Equation

Ruth Klein

With a Foreword by Jay Conrad Levinson, Author of *Guerilla Marketing*

amacom
American Management Association

New York • Atlanta • Boston • Chicago • Kansas City • San Francisco • Washington, D.C.
Brussels • Mexico City • Tokyo • Toronto

Library of Congress Cataloging-in-Publication Data

Klein, Ruth.
    Manage your time/market your business : the time-marketing
equation / Ruth Klein : with a foreward by Jay Conrad Levinson.
        p.   cm.
    Includes bibliographical references and index.
    ISBN 0-8144-0280-1
    1. Time management.   2. Marketing.   3. Success in business.
I. Title.
    HD69.T54K58   1995
    658.8—dc20   95-19362
                                                            CIP

Printing number

10   9   8   7   6   5   4   3   2   1

Contents

Foreword

Let me start out by telling you an enormous lie: Time is money.

The truth is that time is not money. Time is extremely more valuable. If you run out of money, there are many ways to earn more. If you run out of time—well, that's it for you. But you can use time to earn money, no doubt about that. And if you don't know how to use time in that way, you've picked up the perfect book to fill your needs.

Can you actually make money out of thin air? Nope. We both know you can't. Can you actually discover time where you didn't know it existed? You sure can. And it's all over the place, as this book points out. The very concept of *making* time seems impossible—until you read this book.

After reading *Manage Your Time/Market Your Business,* I was very impressed with Ruth Klein's ability to show readers how to *save* time, and even more, how to make the *best use* of their time. Her *Manage Your Time/Market Your Business* is pure genius. As the author of six books on guerrilla marketing, I am knocked out at how she shows readers exactly where to find the time they need to market themselves and their businesses aggressively.

A cornerstone of guerrilla marketing is the need to invest not merely money but *time,* energy, and imagination. Many of you have energy and imagination, but find yourselves short-changed in the area of time. After you complete this book, you'll know exactly where to find the time you need so much.

When I first picked up *Manage Your Time/Market Your Business,* I assumed it would be primarily about time management. Little did I know that it not only contains a multitude of what Ruth calls "Time Tips," but it also is loaded with marketing wisdom—state-of-the-moment marketing tips that can increase any company's profitability—regardless of size.

The book points out that almost everyone has "dead spots" in their day—those times when businesspeople are commuting or talking on the phone or waiting for any one of a vast number of things. What should you do with those dead spots? Fill them with activity, that's what. Recognize that marketing is absolutely all interface between any member of your company and any member of the public, and you quickly realize that dead time can be marketing time, actually converted into profit-producing time that can be used to market your business. For example, while waiting for almost anything, recognize the immense power of thank-you notes to customers. If you do, you'll write a thank-you now. Maybe you'll write ten. Instead of considering that time wasted (as most people would), you'll soon know that it was incredibly valuable time—because you used it wisely.

Manage Your Time/Market Your Business draws on the author's own career in marketing along with many vivid, real-life examples that breathe life into her advice. Instead of turning readers into frenetic Type A behavior zealots, this book shows them that there are ways of saving time, generating profits, and reducing stress—all at the same time. By showing you how to think about marketing, the book guides you through the marketing maze, clarifies an otherwise complex topic, and serves it up to you in a warm, extremely readable manner.

Ruth Klein shows that the names of the marketing game in the 1990s and beyond are *relationships* and *service.* She also is fully aware that it takes time to nurture the customer relationships and render the superlative service. Then, she shows you where to find this time painlessly and effortlessly.

That's even better than showing you where to find money—because money has to be repaid, but time doesn't. Money is something that is often a cause of stress, while time is something that reduces stress. Increasing your marketing power while cutting down on your anxiety is a noble goal for any self-respecting entrepreneur. It doesn't sound easy, but Ruth Klein *makes* it easy. She also makes it realistic.

Her chapters on the media and on trade shows are, all by themselves, worth the price of the book.

Each chapter of *Manage Your Time/Market Your Business* is presented chock full of wise counsel, fascinating insights, lists to keep everything in focus, tales of true-life entrepreneurial adventures, and a concise summary at the end. Ruth wants you to *know* what she knows because she wants you to increase the profits of your company. Her desire for your success is fervent and evident on every page.

With the true spirit of a guerrilla marketer, she alerts you to the proper ways to use marketing weapons, to save money in the process, and to avoid the errors that cause so many small businesses to crash and burn. While she's at it, she's clueing you in on more ways to guard your time and utilize it in a manner that will put a grin on the face of your accountant.

Ruth Klein takes a bold step forward with her innovative hints on discovering time you may not even realize you had and her obvious passion for marketing any size business—from new and teensy to Fortune 500-size. Blended with her knowledge of human behavior and her burning desire for you to beautify your bottom line, she puts at your fingertips the road map to entrepreneurial success that can be used by absolutely anyone in business who is aware of the precious nature of time and the essential need for aggressive marketing.

Jay Conrad Levinson
Author, *Guerilla Marketing*

Acknowledgments

I have had the distinct pleasure of working with many professionally run businesses as clients, which have adopted creative marketing programs resulting from our collective brainstorming. Their faith in my ability as an educator, marketer, and facilitator of time-marketing ideas for their companies is deeply appreciated. The information in this book is a compilation of those experiences. I want to thank those individuals and businesses for making this book possible.

Thanks also go to Duane Newcomb for keeping me on track with my book; Mary Glenn for listening to my ideas; Mike Sivilli for his editorial expertise; Irene Majuk and Karen Wolf for brainstorming new ideas; and Jay Conrad Levinson for believing in the time-marketing message.

However, none of this would be possible without the love, patience, and support of my loving family. To my husband, Alan, for his faith, encouragement, and 100 percent support in all that I do; Naomi, my daughter, who always encourages me in whatever I do; David, my oldest son, who always shares in the excitement of what I'm doing; Daniel, my youngest son, who is always lending a helpful hand in whatever I ask; Shelly and Sarah Gross, my sweet nieces, who remind me of the endless creative possibilities in doing a task.

My wish is for you to pick up at least a few time-marketing tips that you can believe in and that will make the difference to your business's bottom line. Remember: Ideas are only as good as their implementation!

1

The Time-Marketing Equation

Many business people are comfortable telling themselves that their sales are down because of high unemployment, the economy, world events, or the rainy season—in other words, they use any excuse at all. Then how would they explain the fact that others with businesses similar to theirs are recording increased and record-breaking levels of sales?

The answer lies in the Time-Marketing Equation, which means that the amount of time you spend marketing your business is in direct proportion to your bottom line: *profits*.

$$T \times M = X \times P$$

But the time-stressed business person, salesperson, or anyone else must be able to merge the time spent marketing with other business operations, or else he must use the dead spots that occur during every business day, such as coming and going to work, talking on the phone, or waiting for a lunch appointment. Those who learn to do this utilize the key to the Time-Marketing Equation.

Good News for Small Business

These are tough times for small business, yet they are also the best of times. The big news here is that laid-off Fortune 500 employees by the millions have begun establishing their own businesses. While major corporations have cut over 800,000 jobs in the last several years, small business has added more than 350,000 jobs during the same time period. Here are three examples of how laid-off employees have established new careers:

Bert Larsiag, formerly head of the real estate department for a large car parts chain, began a real estate inspection business out of his home. Drawing on his background in construction, insurance claims, and project coordination, he grossed over $50,000 his first year. Currently he has three employees operating out of a small office.

William Teen took early retirement from a large corporation, and sat home for almost two years before he decided to start a Rent-a-Husband service. From the very first he was inundated by calls from professional women who wanted help getting things done around the house. Today, he and four other Rent-a-Husbands operate a very successful business out of a rented garage near his home.

Jamie Krantz, file head when she was laid off from a large corporation, had an obsession with being organized. "When I found myself without a job, I decided to see if I could make a business out of my obsession. Today, she and two other women organize desks and offices, set up off-site storage for businesses, and develop storage systems for closets and kitchens in private homes.

Indicators ranging from those on Wall Street to local newspapers reveal that 85 percent of U.S. businesses employ fewer than twenty-five people and that small business is the fastest-growing segment of the American economy.

Understanding the Time-Marketing Equation

Everything you do in your business, from returning calls to sending out invoices, is a form of marketing. The Time-Marketing Equation implies two things:

1. *The time you take to market your business will be reflected in your bottom line.* You're looking for profit, and effective use of your time leads to profitable marketing.

2. *A time line for your business ideas and goals* will help ensure that action is taken and that specific dates are established for follow-up.

The First Part of the Equation

Much of what I do with clients is to make sure that the ideas and goals we develop together become reality. The time line helps us meet our deadlines. There's more about time lines later in this chapter. Keeping the Time-Marketing Equation in mind, actively position yourself with the following marketing strategies:

Develop an Entrepreneurial Attitude

Attitude is everything. When times get tough, think entrepreneurial; when cash flow is tight, think entrepreneurial; when your customer base changes, think entrepreneurial. To that end, I would like to share my poem with you.

The Entrepreneurial Attitude

I wake up in the morning,
I'm ready to go to work.
I read my favorite paper,
Which is my only perk.

Communication is the name,
That sees my business grow,
I do it everyday,
It keeps my cash a-flow.

My overhead's a burden,
I watch my expenses jump,
I try to keep them down,
My accountant is the "ump."

I have to make decisions,
That are not always for my best,

You have to have an image,
The clients need to know,
It's tougher to communicate,
Than a dog and pony show.

Customer service is a big one,
Follow through is even more,
I try to tell the employees,
"Just do it" or we'll all be poor.

I found a new technique,
They spell it M-A-R-K-E-T-I-N-G,
They say it makes a difference,
Some people charge a fee.

You can have the best ideas,
But it doesn't really mean,

But the company is at stake,	That you're going to have the
And the outcomes are the test.	business,
	Or anything in-between.

Priorities are important,	My business has a vision,
You have to pick and choose,	And a mission statement too,
It isn't always easy,	If only we will follow them,
I think I'll take a snooze.	They may, in fact, come true.

I have to keep on marketing,
And keep it all the same,
So clients know who I am,
And I can play the game.

Be Persistent

Marketing wisdom holds that it takes at least six to eight "hits" before a person or business will be motivated to use your product or service. Your "hit list" might look like this:

1. An article on you and your business appears in the newspaper (providing it's positive). If it's negative, it becomes a negative hit, *and it usually takes four positive hits to make up for each negative hit.*
2. A prospective client meets you at a chamber of commerce meeting or other business function.
3. You call on him/her.
4. Your company sponsors or co-sponsors an event.
5. Word-of-mouth advertising for you and your product/service begins to appear.
6. People read an article that you've written.
7. A prospective client sees one of your advertisements.
8. People see the name of your business "somewhere."

A printing company president says, "Nothing happens until after the *eighth* call. If you make eight calls on a prospect, then it will take someone else at least that many calls to get that prospect away from you."

Keep Your Antennae Up

One of the best ways to know what is going on in your industry, your community, and between your competitors is to listen. When someone suggests a new idea, listen rather than take a judgmental stance as to its effectiveness. Ideas are created because of needs that must be met.

"I did interior design at home," says Madeline Stone of Dallas, "but I was so small I couldn't get people to sell to me at wholesale prices. I contacted suppliers to see if they would sell in small quantities at wholesale. I wound up with hundreds of sources." As she went about her business Madeline began to hear from furniture makers, interior designers, and tailors working on a small scale who could use this information on suppliers. She put together the *Interior Designer Resource Listing*. Over the years this went from a small source book for people who decorate to a mail-order reference guide.

As Madeline discovered, when you keep your antennae up, you often find both answers to your business questions and new opportunities.

TIME TIP: *It takes less time to be attentive to what is happening around you than it does to wander aimlessly.*

Build Business Relationships

Today's business success is dependent on relationships—relationships with your existing clients, with past clients, and with new prospects, as well as with support staff and vendors. You want to do business with *people*, because everything else today is numbers and computers. Chapter 9 discusses business relationships in detail.

TIME TIP: *Nourish your relationships by keeping clients informed of new products or services. Send notes of appreciation, thanking suppliers for information.*

Network

Networking is about sharing information for mutual professional and personal benefit. Effective networking doesn't just happen.

You have to be doing it all the time. In some cases your networking will pay off immediately; in other instances, it may take months or years to see a benefit.

Become a resource for others by connecting people with similar interests. For example, Sandy Thomas, a realtor, gets enjoyment out of matching people for business purposes. She makes a point of jotting down the business needs of people she meets. When she finds someone who can supply these needs, she puts the two parties in touch. Sandy has found that, over the years, this type of networking works well, since many of the people she has helped reciprocate with referrals to her business.

So join associations and clubs that will bring you the greatest visibility, education, enjoyment, and networking opportunities. Approach three new people at each meeting and stay in contact with old friends. Selectively choose your organizations, and move on when the experience is no longer positive. Negative energy is a personal liability. James, an accountant, belonged to a chamber of commerce committee for several years too many: "I would get to the meeting late or leave early and have no time for any meaningful networking. Even while I was there, my mind wondered and I didn't contribute much. I felt my professional image was being hurt—that's when I decided to change committees."

TIME TIP: Join two organizations and become active in each one. Meet three new people at each function. You've taken the time to be at the function; now take advantage of the opportunity.

Make Interesting Conversation

Reading general information as well as that in your area of expertise is an effective marketing tool. Conversations are largely made up of "what's going on"—locally, nationally, and internationally. Share your thoughts.

TIME TIP: If you are shy in social situations, use the 3 × 5 interest card. Write down on the card five interesting things you've read about during the week. Bring the card with you to the function and review it before you mingle. "I feel much more comfortable in social situations with my interest card," says Darren

Sayder, a computer software manager. "I would be very uncomfortable when there was a lull in the conversation. Now, I get the conversation going by using one of the ideas on my card."

Create an Identity Kit

Who are you? What is your business all about? It's vital that you have a basic arsenal or kit that answers these questions.

First, your cards and stationery should have the same logo, phone number, and address on them. Make sure that your identity—humorous, serious, or professional—comes across with every appearance you make, every business card you hand out, every letter you write, and every package you mail. Pass out your business card at every opportunity; this means at meetings, organizations, lunches, and dinners; also follow up any phone calls with a business card.

A Seattle plumber, for instance, called himself "The Barefoot Plumber." He had a picture of a big bare foot painted on both sides of his truck. He placed the image of a bare foot on his cards and stationery, and he erected a sign that extended the barefoot image. Within a few years he was one of the best-known—and busiest—plumbers in the business.

TIME TIP: *Try to order your business cards, stationery, envelopes, and package labels at the same time, especially if there's more than one color in the printing. It takes less time and lowers the cost.*

Develop a High-Powered Mailing List

Put everyone you meet on your mailing list, whether the list be your Rolodex or in a computer database. Write down where you met the person, something you found in common, marital status or children, and whatever the person enjoys doing. Harvey MacKay, in his book *Swim With the Sharks,* has a list of sixty-six items he knows about each of his clients. MacKay's father was in sales and taught Harvey the value of having a database for your customers.[1] If the person you meet has run out of business cards, suggest he or she write down the information on one of your cards.

You don't want an opportunity to walk away. Input the names into your database several times a week.

Go through your database regularly and randomly call five people a day. You may want to say "Hi, haven't seen you for a while. How are things going?" In short, stay in contact with your customers.

TIME TIP: A good time to do your database networking is between 11:30 A.M. and noon, or 4:30 and 5:00 P.M. Rather than "get ready" to go to lunch or home, you train yourself to use this time constructively.

Say Thank-You

Everyone wants to feel appreciated, and most people will do more for someone if they know that their efforts are sincerely appreciated. You can write a thank-you note while you wait for someone to call you back, while you are on hold, or in the few minutes before lunch every day.

Thank-you's come in many forms, but a card is most appreciated and least expensive. Buy all types of cards and postcards—humorous, natural scenes, and cute ones. Having these cards on hand ensures that you will send them out. Most of us have good intentions, but we don't get around to going to the store; then we feel it is too late to write the thank-you, or we just forget. Remember the last time you received a thank-you note? You see—you remember it!

TIME TIP: Saying "thank-you" not only saves you time down the line but eliminates stress. By thanking people for their kind acts, referrals, and so on, we are establishing and maintaining a relationship.

Look for Opportunities

Don't throw anything away until you've glanced at it and asked yourself "How Can I Use This?" Junk mail can present opportunities. I recently received a postcard invitation for an oil-industry trade show. I'm not in the oil industry nor do I have any clients in that field. However, I do give trade show marketing seminars. Listed on the postcard were the address and phone number of the business putting the trade show together. I called the number and spoke to the coordinator, asking her for the names and addresses of past attendees. She could not send me that information, but said she would send me last year's program with the names of businesses and their locations, as well as the current year's program. I would contact these businesses regarding my trade show marketing seminar, which could be presented before their big show.

As you undoubtedly do also, I get all types of brochures. Since I present seminars on many different topics, I don't automatically toss out mail. I review what comes in and look for new ideas to incorporate in my training programs. Why not utilize other people's research? You don't want to reinvent the wheel, although you do want to grease it occasionally or fix a spoke.

Time Tip: If the junk mail brings you something you can use, write down how you plan to use it and act on it or put your note in the appropriate file. It's important that you write down your thoughts before you file something away or set it down. That saves hours of time and frustration later, trying to remember how you were going to use this information.

Challenge the Limits

Just because you've done something a certain way for many years does not mean that that is the way to do it now. New technology, new competition, new consumer attitudes, new regulations, and new problems emerge every day. You need to challenge these limits and ideas. For example, I met with a client recently who works primarily in vocational rehabilitation. After discussing goals, we were able to enlarge the focus of the business to cover the general population. For example, the clients' goals were to (1) increase revenue, (2) expand the range of services offered, and (3) increase existing services to new markets.

This company had been functioning successfully but new regulations came into force and new ways needed to be developed to keep the profits high. By challenging the present limits, we saw the first glimmer of new markets emerge. In the brainstorming exercise, we kept asking the question: What *can* be done differently? The resulting list looked like this:

- Provide a product or service for everyone.
- Expand markets beyond existing territories.
- Increase scope of services and customers.
- Become a primary referral source for insurance and employers.
- Increase the value of rehabilitation.

We agreed that the first item should be the primary focus for the next twelve months. The client gained a new focus and new enthusiasm, and soon had a game plan to reach that goal. The limits of the existing business were challenged and the business expanded.

Watch Your Language

You need to be able to communicate what you do in one sentence, and in simple terms that could be understood by a seventh grader (no technical terms or jargon). Tell people the *results* of what you can do for them. You want the other person to say, "Tell me more about what you do." For example, don't introduce what you do as, "I combine marketing and public relations skills with time management for my clients." That's boring and doesn't really say anything, especially in terms of results for the listener. Instead, say "I'm an educator and motivator who facilitates clients to realize profits in less time."

Introductions in the financial area—accountants, bankers, and stockbrokers—may do the following:

DON'T	"I work for ABC Company."
DO	"I save people money" or "I make money for my clients."

Graphic artist

DON'T	"I'm a graphic artist and I work for ABC company."
DO	"I make your business look good."

Lawyer

DON'T	"I do civil litigation."
DO	"I keep businesses out of legal trouble."

Sales representative

DON'T	"I sell computers."
DO	"I make working with computers easy."

Cosmetologist

DON'T	"I'm a cosmetologist."
DO	"I help people look younger."

Health professional

DON'T	"I work at the ABC medical center."
DO	"I help people live longer."

Helping professions

DON'T	"I'm a therapist."
DO	"I help people enjoy their relationships."

Insurance

DON'T	"I sell insurance."
DO	"I help people enjoy the quality of their life."

The Other Part of the Equation

Why do three out of five new businesses fail? In many cases they lack a solid marketing plan and a time line to reinforce their actions. A marketing strategy is not complete without a time line. Refer to your marketing plan and time line often and revise them as you glean new information.

Let's look at the five steps in a marketing plan and the time line that goes with each.

Step 1: Diagnosis

Where are you right now? Who are you? Describe you, your company, and your employees' traits. Then get your clients or customers to describe you, your company, and your employees. Several important points to consider are:

Personal image	How does each person in the company perceive him or herself, his or her image?
Company image:	How do management, the employees, and clients perceive the company's image?
Employee image:	How do employees view their image?
Competition:	Who is your competition? You may have several competitors for different areas of the business.
Pricing:	How do you determine pricing and what percentage is profit?
Clients:	Who are your existing clients? What are their occupations, ages, marital status, number of children, hobbies, approximate annual salary?
General overhead:	What are your constant costs— telephone, employees, utilities, rent, insurance, travel expenses?
Income source:	Where does 80 percent of your business come from? The Pareto Principle says that 20 percent of your customers bring in 80 percent of your business; 20 percent of your customers bring 80 percent of the complaints.
Repeat business:	How much is repeat business? Who are your repeat customers or clients?

Time Line

Design a time line that covers the following:

Diagnostic Plan   *Date*

1. Diagnostic survey developed   _____
2. Surveys completed internally   _____
3. Surveys completed by clients   _____
4. Results compiled   _____
5. Results analyzed   _____

When you've completed the above, you're ready to go on to Step 2. (The information provided in Step 1 makes an easier and more accurate transition to the next step.)

Step 2: Prognosis

If things continue the way they're going, what can you expect for the future? How can you incorporate the vital research information received in Step 1?

Time Line

Complete the following time line:

Future Plan   *Date*

1. The direction we are headed now   _____
2. New direction(s) we need to take by   _____

You have discovered through this process that there are several directions you want to go. Consider each new idea as a single strategy with its own time line. This is crucial. By developing separate time lines for each strategy, you can realistically pace each.

Step 3: Goals

What are your short-term and long-term goals? Why are you working? Do you love what you do or are you just putting in time? If you're just putting in time, make a change now in the direction of what you enjoy doing.

Time Line

Complete the following time line:

	Date
One-month goal:	_____
Two-month goal:	_____
Three-month goal:	_____
Up to 12-month goal:	Refer to these goals weekly.

Step 4: Strategy

Step 4 divides the doers from the talkers. This is when you put Steps 1,2, and 3 into action. How are you going to get where you want to go? Develop your budget for each strategy—direct mail, telemarketing, advertising, and so on. Start with three strategies and work them. Then go on to other areas.

Time Line

Complete the following time line:

	Development Date	*Implementation Date*
Strategy I	_____	_____
Strategy II	_____	_____
Strategy III	_____	_____

Step 5: Accountability

Step 5 divides those who learn from their marketing plans and those who do not. It's essential to follow up on each strategy to figure out what went well and why, and what did not. This becomes your personal market research. By paying close attention to what worked and what did not, you save effort, time, and money.

Time Line

I suggest immediate follow-up for each strategy listed. Once you've done your follow-ups, analyze what has and has not worked. Remember to look for "real" profits vs. income, image awareness, positioning, and referrals.

Developing a marketing plan and time line is not money-intensive. The plan gives you a road map to follow so that you can reach your business goals by the safest and most economical route.

Summary

The Time-Marketing Equation says that the time you take to market your business will be reflected in your bottom line. Also, you must develop a time line for each of your business ideas and goals. Marketing strategies that actively position you and your business include developing an entrepreneurial attitude, being persistent, keeping your antennae up, building business relationships, networking, making interesting conversation, creating an identity kit, developing a high-powered mailing list, saying thank-you, looking for opportunities, challenging the limits, and watching your language.

Your marketing plan and time line reinforce your business decisions. The five steps in the plan include diagnosis, prognosis, goals, strategy, and accountability.

Note

1. Harvey MacKay, *Swim With the Sharks Without Being Eaten Alive* (New York: William Morrow & Co., 1988).

2

Connecting and Reconnecting With Your Customers

Remember the United Airlines ad in which the company president tells his sales personnel that its biggest customer of twenty-five years just fired the company? And what was the reason? "We no longer know you." All recent contact had been via the phone or fax. So it's no wonder the airline felt the agency was a stranger.

Outside pressures and technological changes demand our attention and interest in the business world. How can you keep attuned to trends and yet stay focused on your business? The answer lies in looking within—in connecting and reconnecting. You must find creative ways to connect and reconnect in very personal ways with all your customers.

Time-Marketing Connections

When Bob Jones and his partner finished breakfast at a small restaurant in Carmel, California, the busboy asked how the food was. Bob answered, "good" and his partner said "OK." Next thing they knew, the cook was at their table and asking them where they were from. A pleasant conversation followed. But rather than start the conversation negatively with "I heard your breakfast was not good," the cook had begun a congenial chat with both patrons. This way he would not have to offer a free meal next time. Both Bob and his partner would go back to the restaurant again and would also suggest the place to others. They left with a positive impression even though the meal wasn't outstanding.

Let's look at the Time Marketing that went on:

- The staff is told to let the cook or someone else know if a patron is not pleased about something. Management has taken the time to train and follow up on this point.
- The cook takes time away from his regular work to chat with customers who are not 100 percent pleased.
- The cook remained positive in his conversation, never asking what was wrong.
- The cook did not have to give away a free meal or deduct anything from the bill because he had connected positively with the clients. The cook made time to save a paying customer.

TIME TIP: *Make time to satisfy your customers, who in turn will market your business for you. That marketing equals profit to your business.*

A Client-Centered Culture

The key concept here is to connect and reconnect with your clients. Let's look at nine ways to do this in a time-efficient way.

Stay in Contact

One of the best ways to keep your customers and clients is to stay in contact with them. Joanne Senders, district sales manager of an insurance company, says an "effective sales approach I use is constantly staying in touch with the people I call on."

I work mostly with busy professionals; however I know how important making these weekly "connections" are. I set up weekly or biweekly appointments with my clients, whether in person or over the phone. An analysis of my client list over the years has shown that the clients I consistently kept in contact with are the ones who are still my clients today. Another way to say this is, even clients who are happy with your marketing and public relation efforts will not stay with you without regular contact.

Many years ago I learned this the hard way. Among my clients, I had one who made in excess of $4 million annually. The company had called me in when one of the partners left and took a few assistants with him. Some of the marketing and public relations we provided for the company included a name change, a new logo and updated image, a brochure, an open house with 3-D tours, a press conference with television and print coverage, and several articles in the local newspaper (one half-page in color). I worked with them for nine months, but in the last two months I did not make the time to meet with them. I felt I had accomplished a lot for the client and did not think it necessary to keep up weekly contact. When I finished the project, the company dropped me.

TIME TIP: No matter how much you have done for your client, you must stay connected.

My favorite Time Marketing metaphor is a car. You can wash your car everyday and keep it covered when not in use, but when the gas is gone the car won't run, no matter how "happy" it is to be clean and protected. You must keep fuel in the tank.

Go Beyond What the Customer Wants

Satisfying the customer or client today is not enough because competitors are always waiting to fill in the gaps. The key is to go beyond what the customer wants. Customers buy products and services based on emotion, and they support these emotional buying habits with logic. This is true for everything we purchase. A business needs an accountant and an attorney, but its managers select them based on wants and emotions—the people they find most likeable, credible, intelligent, or service-oriented.

A local food market, for instance, offers rotating specials. The store might offer 20 percent off on all the products in an entire aisle for fifteen minutes, four or five times a day. Customers never know what items will be reduced, but the approach is novel so many people come in just to see what they can save on that day. The clerks always have a smile, every customer cashing a check gets addressed by name, and all are thanked for shopping at the store. This sales approach goes beyond what any other store in the area offers. It gives customers more than they ask for, in an emotionally satisfying way.

TIME TIP: *You must market every day, with everyone, everywhere you go. It takes less time to be pleasant, flexible, and helpful than it does to be unpleasant, inflexible, and aggressive.*

One of my clients recently said to me at lunch, "Ruth, you were nurturing, helpful, and so giving even before we did business together." This client calls me to do a project in excess of $4,000 every year. Going beyond the ordinary is definitely part of the Time-Marketing Equation.

A stockbroker client in the business for over twenty years works on some of the most complex trades ever done. He says, "I am selling service and expertise." But he is wrong! He is selling himself first, and his services and expertise second. People may have found you likeable, trustworthy, friendly, sincere, or credible. Once you have "sold" them on you, then—and only then—can you approach them with your products or services. For example, I worked with a CPA on the board of a nonprofit organization. I was impressed with his knowledge of accounting and his likeable personality. As a result, I am seriously considering him as my business accountant.

Go Beyond What the Customer Expects

Unfortunately, we are living in a time when "customer service" is more lip service than real service. When a salesperson, doctor, lawyer, or plumber does a job the way it should be done, when the person is pleasant as well, we are impressed. But leading-edge companies have figured this out and always give customers *more* than they expect. When you go beyond their expectations, customers feel loyalty toward you and your products. They feel special in return.

TIME TIP: *It takes less time to take care of your customer initially than to try and "make up" for poor service if and when something goes wrong. It takes less time to give customers more than they expect than to offer the "add-on" later.*

Build Relationships via Communications

Marketing is all about communicating your services or products to every person you work with—customers, vendors, dealers, support staff, employees, and employers. Communication is the key to marketing:

Communication = marketing = profits.

There are several types of communication, however.

Internal Communication

First and foremost, you need to communicate your image. Do you want others to perceive you as humorous, dependable, professional, credible, easy-going, or friendly? For example, a court-reporting business deals with attorneys in suits and ties all day. Yet the owner takes pride in the fact that her company is friendly and easy-going: "I feel flattered when an attorney comes into the office, he loosens or completely takes off his tie." This is a case where the court reporter's personal image is consistent with her business image. If the two are not perceived as consistent by others, then it is difficult to reach out to new clients or keep old ones.

You reflect your business image through your employees, office furnishings, personal dress, and everything you do. For instance, a residential and business security company has its business in a restored older home in the downtown area. As you walk into its office, you are greeted with comfortable furniture in a very warm setting.

I love shopping at Nordstrom's Department Store because of its piano music. Shopping at Nordstrom's is a calming experience. I also enjoy doing research at the SBA's Small Business Development Center because all its employees are helpful and cheerful. The business images of these companies come through loud and clear.

Customer Communication

Tony Alessandra and Phil Hunsaker, in their book, *Communicating at Work,* present four dimensions of behavior: Direct, Indirect, Supporting, and Controlling.[1] They describe a Direct person as fast-paced, assertive, take-charge, forceful, risk confronting, outspoken, impatient, and thriving on accomplishment. An Indirect person is one who is more cautious in attitude toward risk and decision making, is slower paced, more low-key, tentative, and a reserved communicator.

A typical Supporting person is emotionally open, uses animated facial expressions, tends to be a hugger and toucher, prefers informal and relaxed relationships, and is a feeling-oriented decision maker. And the Controlling person tends to be emotionally reserved, more rigid with expression, task- and fact-oriented, follows more rigid plans and schedules, and is more comfortable communicating in an intellectual setting.

It is important to realize what type of customer you are working with so that you can accommodate your business for his or her communication style—vocally, visually, and verbally. For example, if you're a Supporting person speaking to a Controlling person, you will want to discuss the task at hand and not talk about personal issues.

Investigative Communication

Ask your customers. Find out what the competition is doing. Use the ideas from your reading and those you get at conferences. Investigate your markets by subscribing to the trade journals. One newsletter can give you a wealth of ideas and information. Look at the advertisers and products in the magazine, too.

Database Communication

Think of your client or customer database as part of your inventory. If used effectively, it is worth hundreds of thousands of dollars to you in the lifetime of your business. I have not found a way to keep all my client information in my head. Writing it down or putting it into a database helps keep my mind clear for new ideas.

TIME TIP: *The best time to get information about your customers is during the first few times you get together. This is when a lot of "sharing" goes on. And update your database as new information comes along.*

Develop a Newsletter

An estate attorney had several hundred clients and many prospects. Not knowing how to keep in contact with these people caused him anxiety. He felt he was losing business as well. Likewise, a realtor who had been in business over twenty years was no longer getting the listings she thought she deserved. Several of her "old" clients were listing with other realtors. During holidays, she kept in contact with recent clients, but not older ones.

In both cases my company started a personalized newsletter for the clients that went out to everyone on their databases— clients, potential clients, and people whom they met in organizations and at meetings, names from newspaper articles, and so on. A personalized newsletter incorporates the personality of the sender and keeps people in touch. For example, the attorney likes to tell jokes and the realtor is interested in health matters, so we sprinkled jokes throughout the attorney's newsletter and created a health column in the realtor's.

Some important points to remember when creating a newsletter are:

- Keep the newsletter personal.
- Add a section or two about your interests that coincide with those of many of your customers—health topics, sports, jokes, home maintenance, garden ideas, tax and financial tips.
- Mix print with graphics in an eye-pleasing format.
- Bullet your main ideas and keep the amount of reading down.
- Use a second color to enhance the impact.

- Use an 11 × 17-inch folded format—it is easy to use and read.
- Place your phone number in conspicuous places.
- Include artwork and photos. People love looking at pictures. Make sure your shining face appears with a message at the beginning or at the end.

We write several newsletters for our clients, and each one takes approximately eight to ten hours to assemble. The expense of printing 1,000 newsletters and mailing them third class is approximately $500, not including the cost of graphics.

TIME TIP: If you have several hundred clients, you can still create a newsletter that communicates your ideas, products, or services, with your voice and personality. Jot down the ideas and outsource the copy, graphics, printing, and mailing. Remember, outsource as many activities and duties as can be done by others and do only those that an owner does best—marketing.

Treat Your Customer as Your Partner

Sharon Cupp, a leading broker in residential sales that topped $22 million in 1992, says, "I have discovered the long-term value of good rapport with clients. For me, rapport combined with persistence not only gets me in the door but helps keep me there."

The owners of Ben & Jerry's claim they developed "a connection with our customers that went beyond that achieved by traditional advertising and promotions." The two men started factory tours in 1986, and five years later the tours had become the "largest tourist attraction in the state of Vermont, drawing over 225,000 paid admissions for the year."[2]

> With paid advertising, we had ten seconds or a momentary scan of a page, in among the clutter of other ads and the medium's editorial content, to capture the consumer's attention. . . . On the tours, we had the rapt attention of our customers for over an hour, which afforded us an unparalleled opportunity to educate visitors on our company's history, products, and business philosophy.[3]

Patty DeDominic, owner of PDQ Personnel Services, Inc., and current national president of National Association of Women Business Owners (NAWBO), sent a letter and flyer to her clients and association members describing a contest PDQ was sponsoring to celebrate its fifteenth anniversary. The company wanted "to share some of our success with those people who have given credibility to the positive role that 'temps' fulfill—those folks who have gone 'on assignment.' " It never ceases to amaze me, as I meet company presidents and organization leaders, how many people have had temp-job experiences. This agency's contest is another example of a beautiful tie-in, connecting and reconnecting with clients.

TIME TIP: **Keep in contact with your customers quarterly—at a minimum. Create excitement and energy for your business by offering a contest, tour, or yearly birthday party, with your customers as the focus.**

Sponsor an Annual Event

Most people love going to parties where they can relax, enjoy good company, enjoy good food and music, and possibly network. Most people also feel comfortable with repetition, because they know what to expect and a tradition is relished. All this adds up to sponsoring an annual event.

The law firm of O'Neil & Widelock takes advantage of the Irish descent of Gary O'Neil and the type of law—adoptions—that Marc Widelock practices. The law firm puts on a yearly St. Patrick's Day buffet dinner at the office. Irish stew, soda bread, Irish truffles, and several types of beer make up the annual menu. Gary wears the traditional kilt all day, including when he's in court and with clients, and the bagpipes are a hit with clients, prospects, and the media.

Likewise, since the firm is one of the largest handling adoptions in California's Central Valley, every November (National Adoption Month) it sponsors an annual Adoption Forum. This year the forum tropic was "How to Parent the Adopted Child"; yearly updates are also given on laws affecting adoptions. The previous year, the firm presented a seminar by three birth-mothers, one birth-father, and a public-adoption counselor. Marc Widelock was the facilitator or, as he says, "I was Phil Donahue." The firm received media coverage on both sponsored events. In a similar vein, a few years back O'Neil & Widelock represented only men in family law issues, so they sponsored an annual Father's Day picnic.

TIME TIP: *Think of sponsoring a party once a year for your customers, prospects, and the media. In many instances, sponsoring the event will take less time and cost less money than putting together a quarterly newsletter.*

Conduct Customer Surveys

Customer surveys are a great way to find out about your company. The first thing is to decide the *purpose* of the survey—What results do you want? We developed a survey for a vocational-rehabilitation counseling company. The purpose was "finding out what clients think about the services, and letting them know the number of certified vocational counselors available." We brainstormed what the company would like to know, and the preliminary list looked like this:

- Is there anything that would discourage you from using our services?
- Do you rate us as excessive or reasonable in cost?
- Timeliness?
- Quality?
- Outcome?
- Happy with documentation?
- Professional?
- Communication skills?
- Are we objective?
- How would you rate our counseling skills?
- Would you like case-tracking reports?
- Are there any reasons you would not use them?
- Of the six certified counselors, how many have you worked with?
- Are you aware of geographic areas we cover?
- How many cases a year do you have?

We had a choice. We could mail the surveys and hope to get responses, or we could randomly call ten to fifteen clients and ask them the questions over the phone. In addition, we would selectively (not randomly) choose a few clients for their feedback. We would keep the results of these two surveys separate.

The decision was made to call clients. The transcript of the survey we developed was as follows:

> Good morning [afternoon]. My name is Ruth Klein and I am calling for [name of client]. I would like to ask you five questions and it shouldn't take more than five minutes of your time. [Go straight into asking the first survey question.]
>
> 1. Do you feel the certified vocational counselors at [client's name] are professional? [We expected a yes answer here to get respondents into a positive frame of mind.]
> 2. Of the six certified vocational counselors at [name of client], how many have you worked with? Would you work with them again? [Keep repeating the name of the company and their strong feature (six certified vocational counselors)].
> 3. Do you feel the counselors are unbiased and objective?
> 4. Are the fees excessive or reasonable?
> 5. How could [name of business] help you further? [An open-ended question at the end allows the respondent to express other thoughts about the company.]

Here are some points to remember when developing a survey:

- Keep it brief. Ask only three to five questions.
- Make each question count. Each response needs to answer a specific question you have—customer service, cost, quality, and so on.
- One of the first questions should obtain a yes answer. This gets the person answering the survey in a position to answer more questions.

- Repeat the name of the business often.
- Stress the strength of the business or its employees in the way the questions are phrased—for example, six certified vocational counselors. This shows contrast—most of the competitors are smaller and employees are not as well qualified.
- Be consistent. Write out a script and ask the same questions of all respondents.
- Thank your respondents for their time.
- Analyze written or verbal responses.

With your customer surveys developed, implemented, and analyzed, put this valuable market research into your database. Save time by asking questions that will get answers you can easily input and ultimately use to determine customer likes and dislikes.

TIME TIP: Customer surveys are a way to keep in contact with your customers. The more information they receive from you, the more they remember who you are and what you do. Sending surveys once a year shows that you care and that you're constantly improving, and it acts as a reminder about your business.

Develop Your Database—An Additional Profit Center

It's important to insert information from every business card you receive at business meetings and social gatherings, and from every prospective client, vendor, media person, and present client you speak to. A well-maintained and up-to-date database can earn you extra money by partnering your business with other businesses that share common demographics and psychographics.

For example, a computer billing company targeted local lawyers and doctors for their services. They developed a mailing list of these names and now sell this special list to other companies that want to target lawyers and doctors for their businesses. "When we meet a business person who wants to target the legal or medical profession, we sell them our updated lists," states the owner. "The money we receive from these lists has gone directly into buying more software."

Summary

To stay in tune with your customers you need to continuously connect and reconnect with them. Nine time-efficient ideas are to stay in contact weekly or biweekly, go beyond what the customer wants, go beyond what the customer expects, build relationships via communications, develop a newsletter, treat your customer as a partner, sponsor an annual event, conduct customer surveys, and develop your database.

Notes

1. Tony Alessandra and Phil Hunsaker, *Communicating at Work* (New York: Simon & Schuster, 1993).
2. Ben Cohen and Jerry Greenfield, *Ben & Jerry's: The Inside Scoop* (New York: Crown, 1994).
3. Ibid.

3

Understanding Customer Lifestyles

Advertising agencies call it "marketing with psychographics." It means marketing directly to a customer's lifestyle, such as baby boomers, the mature market, newly marrieds, and so on rather than only looking to age, sex, income, or other demographics. It also means that each family in a particular neighborhood might have completely different buying habits because of a different lifestyle. Today, a business *must* know the lifestyle needs of its customers in order to market with any efficiency.

The Time-Marketing Equation implies that a company that wants to be competitive in the 1990s and beyond must follow the lifestyle trends and market choices of different groups of customers. It also implies that this marketing activity must be sandwiched between other business activities and take a minimum of time.

The Importance of Trends

Trends are very important for business. The owner of a printing business that grosses over $5 million dollars—about nineteen times the industry average (more about this in Chapter 7)—spends a great deal of time reading about trends in population, economics, and otherwise. "He's a very dynamic, aggressive marketer. He watches trends, and he tries new things," says one of his printing pals.

Faith Popcorn, in her book, *The Popcorn Report*, says "The trends take off your blinders. They open up your eyes—and give you TrendVision. And that's the only way to see the future coming."[1]

The Importance of Lifestyle

People generally are classed by age, for trends and lifestyles seem to follow generations as they age.

Baby Boomers

Arriving after World War II, these people were born between 1946 and 1964 and constitute 78 million Americans. They are the largest generation in American history. They are also the first TV and atomic generation. They witnessed what taking drugs can do firsthand; they lost a president to assassination and forced another president to resign in disgrace. Generally they have two-career families and had children later than previous generations. And their savings record is not good. This group has confused demographers with its size, degree of affluence, level of education, politics, and feminist outlook. At one point, some baby boomers were referred to as yuppies—young urban professionals. Demographers are now calling yuppies "grumpies," for grown-up mature professionals.

Manufacturers are developing new products like wide-seated jeans, frilly girdles, and expensive bifocals that do not show the telltale lines in the lenses. RJR Nabisco introduced miniature Oreos, intended to give baby boomers a nostalgic taste with reduced calories and guilt. Haagen-Dazs recently added a smaller ice-cream bar.

The baby-boom generation wants to stay young and healthy, so it fights every extra pound and extra year. As one television ad says, "I'm not going to grow old gracefully." Fitness and health foods are popular with the aging baby boomers. So the products and services that cater to the changing lifestyles of this group will be the ones that show profits. As this population grays, marketing efforts for clothing, foods, restaurants, fitness, and travel should be accelerating. This mature, soon-over-50 market accounts for 43 percent of all households and half of all discretionary income.

Trends

- Because baby boomers are fighting the "sagging effect," plastic surgery is predicted to triple in the next decade.
- There will be an increase in consumer affluence.
- Baby boomers will take their political power with them into their graying years.
- Because of their large numbers, baby boomers have the power to make their behavior—any behavior—the norm.

Generation X

The so-called generation X (born between 1959 and 1974) is beginning to have a greater impact on the U.S. economy as this age group marries and begins to raise children. Not as populous as the baby boomers, generation X has its own lifestyle that you must take into account if you expect business from this group. Its impact will be felt significantly in the years to come.

Recent research found that 87 percent of generation X men and women were completely satisfied with the demands of their jobs, and that 87 percent had a strong sense of company loyalty; 69 percent believed that people get ahead by their own hard work. They are essentially more conservative than the baby boomers, and are more hard-fisted with their money.

The average full-time salary for a male between the ages of 25 and 34 is $26,197. The average for a female is $21,510. About 46 percent of the single "twentysomethings" still live with mom and dad.

Here are some generation X facts: The proportion of men age 20 to 22 who marry is on the rise. This reflects a rise in income, making them more open to taking on the expense of a home—and making them a larger market than before for independent retailers.

Most babies are being born to young married couples, another clue to the fact that this generation has some money to spare. Thanks to low interest rates, homeownership among people in their twenties turned upward in 1993, after thirteen years of decline. And this generation will be a larger market for all types of products and information in the future. Anyone attempting to market to this group should become aware of their differences, and market directly to this younger audience through personal contact, direct mail, or radio.

Baby Busters

The generation born between 1965 and 1976 represents a large portion of the U.S. population. In fact, this group is larger than the population of existing senior citizens. The American baby-bust generation is 44 million strong.

As a consumer group, baby busters spend $200 billion each year—more than all previous averages on clothes, music, sports gear, and electronics.

Trends

- Baby busters leave home later and marry later than did earlier generations.
- Baby busters' savings and disposable income are much greater than those of earlier generations.
- Baby busters are prime consumers for big-ticket items such as cars, computers, electronics, clothing, travel, and home furnishings.

Your marketing should keep in mind that products previously bought by established married couples in their thirties may no longer be relevant to a singles group that consumes according to want, not necessarily need. Your business may need to shift attention toward creating desire, rather than necessity.

Putting the Lifestyle System to Work

Let's look at a couple ways businesses can market to the various lifestyles and spend no more time doing it than usual.

Home Mortgages

Banks and mortgage companies that take lifestyle into account give borrowers a choice of mortgages. For example, fixed-rate mortgages are loans paid off in equal monthly installments over the term of the loan. Adjustable-rate mortgages are loans whose interest rates can change according to the money market. Their amortization schedule is periodically readjusted for these changes; therefore monthly payments can vary from year to year. Graduated-payment mortgages are loans in which monthly payments are increased annually by a certain percentage over the first several years, and then become fixed for the remaining term of the loan. Growing-equity mortgages are loans with monthly payments that increase significantly each year according to a set schedule or a preselected index.

Religion and Personal Preferences

According to a survey conducted by Princeton Survey Research Associates, "faith in God is the most important part of Americans' lives, followed by good health and a happy marriage." According to the report, 40 percent of respondents said they "valued their relationship with God above all else, while only 2 percent said a job that pays well was the most important thing in their lives."[2] Where did the baby boomers go, demographers are asking? Something is going on in the culture shift. In addition to the 40 percent who said faith in God was what they valued most, 29 percent cited good health and 21 percent said a happy marriage was most important. For many people, this is a long-held fact of American life.

Businesses can use this trend information. For example, enrollment in secular schools is on the rise; clothes stores will be selling more "church" attire to the entire family; bookstores would be wise to carry books on religion and values; volunteering for good "causes" will be on the upswing as well as baby boomers mature.

What Today's Shoppers Want

Demographics aside, today's shoppers are a completely different breed.

Trends

- Shoppers invest significant research and energy in each purchase by shopping around, comparing prices and features.

- They demand higher quality and better service and are stocking up on higher-value goods.
- They do more bargaining, use more coupons, and buy more at discount stores.
- They prefer stores that offer value-added services such as free repairs, complaint departments, assembly services.
- They believe they can buy 90 percent of their purchases anywhere.
- They seek out stores that are organized to make shopping easier and faster.

The merchandiser who provides shoppers with easy access to product information, offers support services, and has a well-organized store will pull in a good share of these sales. Sell the sizzle and provide a good-quality steak!

The Family Unit

American society is entering a powerful family-oriented period that will see spouses, children, and seniors consuming as a unit.

Trends

- Marketing efforts that utilize interpersonal hopes and fears of family relationships will have a large impact on buying decisions.
- Research shows that word-of-mouth product recommendations from one family member to another are more effective than comments made between friends.

Develop a marketing plan that brings in a "full-family" marketing approach, drawing in spouses, children, and seniors.

Lifestyle and the Time-Marketing Equation

There is no reason to reinvent the wheel—you'll find a great deal of information out there already. Regularly read three or four newsletters and magazines that are easy to follow, offer helpful information, and from which you can glean the most important facts quickly. You can find such trade publications at the library. While reading, stay alert to sources cited and recommended readings. The more I look for information, the more impressed I become. There is a source for almost anything you would want to know.

Recognizing lifestyle trends will give you a headstart on developing new products, adding services, or modifying what already exists. Wayne Gretzky, celebrity hockey player, once said in an interview as to why he does so well: "When I get on the ice and play begins, everyone else on the ice goes where the puck is. Me? I go where the puck is going to be." That's why looking at trends in any industry or at the interests of specific targeted populations is an excellent start. Trends do not guarantee the way things will be, but if you consistently review these trends, you can pick up ideas that will help your business grow.

Here are some more trends:

- Two-thirds of all buying decisions are made in-store, making point-of-purchase one of the most influential ways to reach consumers.
- Women account for 80 percent of all consumer spending in the United States. Seventy percent of women are employed, 59 percent are married, 61 percent have at least a high school diploma, 58 percent have no children under the age of 18 living at home.
- Sales of kosher foods are rising at a brisk pace, a trend related to interest in healthy and nutritious food. Kosher food sales are estimated at more than $32 billion a year, with a growth rate annually of 15 percent. (Kosher certification requires that kosher meats come from animals raised without growth-stimulating chemicals.)
- By the year 2000, the 40-plus age group will control over 75 percent of America's wealth.
- Seventy-five percent of women's health-care decisions are made by women.
- Disabled Americans make up a larger population group

than either Hispanics or blacks, and their numbers are increasing.

- Children between the ages of 4 and 12 spend approximately $9 billion of their own money and influence $130 billion in adult spending.

Direct-Target Marketing

The term "market research" can be intimidating to the small-business owner. One immediately thinks of big dollars, fancy computer software, and large research teams. But there is an abundance of information you can use for your own market research. A telephone call or letter asking for more information is a good place to start. For example, the Small Business Association (SBA) offers the pamphlet "Researching Your Market (MT 8)," which can be ordered for $1 from SBA Publications, P.O. Box 30, Denver, CO 80201-0030. The SBA, together with Bell Atlantic, sells a videotape called "Marketing: Winning Customers with a 'Workable' Plan." To order the tape, send a check for $30 to the SBA Marketing Video, Department A, P.O. Box 30, Denver, CO 80201-0030.

Published market research surveys are also helpful. Take advantage of the expensive surveys funded by others. Find/SVP, a private research company in New York City, publishes a bimonthly information catalog of more than 8,000 market research reports, studies, and surveys available from hundreds of publishers, covering thirty-seven industries. Prices range from as low as $50 to several thousand dollars.

But the most important thing to remember about market research is who your customer is. When I started my marketing company I worked with a lot of small businesses. After eighteen months, I looked closely at my clients and discovered some valuable market information for my company. I listed my clients and everything I knew about them—approximate age, hobbies, how they enjoyed spending their leisure time, annual income, married or single, how many years married or single, products or services they purchased from me, type of music they liked, what part of the country they were in during their formative years (ages 2–14).

I found that my clients were mostly entrepreneurs, professionals, and authors. They had my same profile: I had been the entrepreneur in a women's dress shop and was now a marketing and public relations professional. I had a master's degree in clinical psychology, and I was an author. The way I want to spend my time is similar to the way my clients want to spend their time. I now know exactly who my clients are and how to target this lifestyle group.

For example, if your target customers are upscale retail consumers, you need to provide style, quality, store ambience, marketing, and pricing that mesh with their lifestyle. Personal invitations work well for this.

Recently, a health-care facility personally invited executives and business owners to a luncheon during Public Health Week. I felt special after reading the first nine words of the invitation: "Your presence is kindly requested at a special luncheon. . . ." They wanted *me* to be there, not along with everyone else. That fits my perception of being important enough to take the time to go.

Talk With Your Clients and Customers

Keep tabs on information your customers and employees give you. Randomly ask your customers questions—how they feel about family life or politics; what they think is happening locally; how well they like your product or service and how your product or service could be better; and anything else you would like to know. Write it down.

Also, try this research approach: Ask seven customers the same question and chances are you will spot a trend. Whenever I am asked to give a speech, I contact seven people who will be in the audience and I ask them three questions. More times than not, a concern emerges that I can use to tailor my speech.

Check Out Your Competition

Looking at the competition is always a good idea when you put together your market research. There are a number of ways to do this. For example, examine ads in trade publications, attend industry seminars and trade shows, visit the competitor's store, talk to the competitor's customers, and examine their brochures and catalogs.

In trying to understand today's customer, don't forget the time factor. All consumers are short on time. Professional women particularly are stressed trying to juggle home, family, and job. But many workers today put in eight to ten extra hours each week just to keep up. You probably do too. So small businesses that remember this, and that make sure their products or services save customers' time, will stay ahead of the competition.

Summary

It is essential today that businesses market to their customers' lifestyles. New trends give important information on how to reach these customers or clients. Baby boomers make up the largest group in America, and their likes and dislikes differ from those of the baby bust and generation X groups.

Get familiar with your customers' likes and dislikes and watch your competitors also. Use available information on lifestyles and trends to effectively market to your customers.

Notes

1. Faith Popcorn, *The Popcorn Report,* (New York: Bantam Doubleday Dell, 1991). Copyright © 1991 by Faith Popcorn. Used by permission of Doubleday, a division of Bantam Doubleday Dell Publishing Group, Inc.
2. Princeton Survey Research Associates, telephone survey of 600 adults conducted in New York City, January 17–20, 1995, for the Lifetime television show "The Great American TV Poll."

4

Finding the Uniqueness in Your Business

Customers often do business with a company because of something extra that the company offers. Managers need to ask themselves: What are we providing that offers the customer a unique service or experience? A retailer who offers an "unconditional" lifetime guarantee on every item has one-upped his or her competition. Customers just want "a little attention, a little recognition of the no-one's-quite-like-me type. It's about individuating, differentiating, customizing. And it's a major force to reckon with in today's marketplace," says Faith Popcorn, in *The Popcorn Report.*[1]

The company that best develops products, programs, and services to promote the customer's feeling of being unique will be most successful. For example, my children enjoy going to restaurants where they receive free desserts on their birthday. My daughter likes an out-of-town restaurant that gives one-quarter of a triple-layered chocolate cake for dessert on a customer's birthday.

Faith Popcorn coined the term *Egonomics.* "Egonomics means simply this: there is a profit to be reaped in providing for the consumer's need for personalization—whether it be in product concept, product design, 'custom ability,' or personal service."[2]

William R. Carey, Jr., founder and chief executive of Corporate Resource Development, Inc., in Atlanta, agrees:

> I went broke as a commodity company, a company that didn't try to distinguish itself from all the other companies in our market. I remember the three questions I used to be asked that gave me the chance to declare my generic intentions.

"What kind of business are you in?"
We're in the training business.
"What kind of training do you do?"
Any kind.
"Whom do you do it for?"
Anybody who'll buy. How about you? I can be there
in the morning.[3]

Carey says, "Your end-user will have to believe that your product
or service is different from and more valuable than the other products in your market." He calls this process "brand identity" and
feels that no company is too small to develop it. Carey suggests an
easy way to successfully master the idea of brand identity:[4]

- Understand what makes your product or service special.
- Understand your product or service well enough to be able
  to describe it clearly.
- Value your brand so much that people are willing to pay
  more for whatever it is that makes it special.
- Feel so strongly about your brand that your customer will
  defend it—even at a higher price.

We're in an information and technological age when so much
of our identity is differentiated by numbers. Rupert Murdoch's
News Corporation feels it is important in an information age to
narrowcast. Creating a certain uniqueness in your business caters
to customers internally, at an emotional level. Since buying is
largely an emotions-driven activity, the "good feeling" accompanied by differentiation and personalization is a plus.

Because consumers want to find and relate to other people like
themselves, all types of "narrow casted" groups are forming, from
the personal to the political. This uniqueness turns into strength
with greater numbers and fellow bonding. For example, many
businesses create uniqueness by creating something that has been
lost or restoring a memory, filling multipurpose needs, raising the
ante, being the low-cost provider, being flexible, or using all the
senses.

Recreating or Restoring Something That Has Been Lost

Health and Wellness

Customers are concerned with their own and their families' health and safety. The more we learn about what is happening to our water and food, the more caution we take. Many shoppers are triumphant when they can purchase foods that say in bold print, "no preservatives" or "all natural." Tom's of Maine products boldly claim no saccharin, no preservatives, no dyes, no animal ingredients, and all natural flavors.

Businesses that introduce products and services that recreate a feeling of health and wellness for the consumer ultimately benefit from this type of uniqueness. At one time, Tom's of Maine toothpaste could be found only in health food or specialty stores. Today, you can pick it up in most supermarkets.

Meditation, an old Eastern method to reduce stress, has become a mainstream interest. Vitamins to ensure health and energy have also made a strong impact.

Old-Fashioned Customer Service

The "back to basics" idea is gaining steam in many areas, such as health, personal relationships, food, and customer service. Back-to-basics customer service is what Barry Steinberg's East Coast Direct Tire business is all about, even though "on average we are consistently 10 percent or 12 percent higher than just about everybody," says Barry.

If you need to be out of his shop within an hour, no problem because you can schedule an appointment when it's convenient for you, not the shop. If you can't wait for your car, then you can take one of the company's seven loaners to work and pick yours up on the way home. Plus, "if your tires blow out after 30,000 miles or you decide after a month that you flat out don't like them, no sweat." Steinberg guarantees the tires, as well as any service work his shop does—forever. In addition to his unique service, he posts twice the industry average on sales of over $4 million.

A locally owned grocery store and deli in California, in a small space by grocery store standards, makes in excess of $2 million annually and encourages charge accounts. The deli itself has an old-time look. There are barrels everywhere, piled high with the raw ingredients to make hundreds of kinds of ethnic foods. Italian cooks can buy ten different kinds of beans in bulk from the barrels, take home seven kinds of basil found hanging from a wire at the back of the store, and buy more kinds of pasta than customers realized existed.

It also features warm ethnic dishes, especially Italian and Mexican, carefully prepared with fresh vegetables and fresh herbs. The bakery sells authentic Austrian-style pastries. Customers are urged to sample the prepared ethnic deli dishes that line every counter. A small section at the back features several hundred cookbooks, a pot-bellied stove, a table, and chairs where customers can rest. Customers flock to the store because it is such a throwback to another time and is so different from anything else in the city.

Restoring a Memory

Some customers want to go back to a time when there were fewer choices and a simpler, less hectic lifestyle. Past years often seem to have been easier to people than present years are. Certain past decades are thought of affectionately, particularly the 1950s for their rock 'n roll and the 1960s as the hippie era. The chain of Hard Rock Cafes has done a beautiful job in helping to bring back the uniqueness in certain memories.

Likewise, coffeehouses have sprung up across the nation as representative of the uniqueness of the 1960s. Bed and breakfast inns have discovered a way to restore the feeling of being home with family and friends while away.

Many cities have "older" areas that were once thriving cornerstones of the community. Sacramento, California, restored several blocks of its riverfront as Old Sacramento, built in the 1850s, during the gold rush era. Businesses that moved in there included a number of gourmet restaurants and toy and candy stores. Located there also is the *Delta Queen* riverboat that plied the Sacramento River during gold rush days, and a state railroad museum featuring rolling stock and steam engines dating back to the early days.

During the Memorial Day weekend, the Sacramento Jazz Festival, held in Old Sacramento, features over 120 traditional jazz bands from around the world, making it the largest jazz festival and attracting crowds of over 200,000.

Recently, there was a celebration around such an old California city, centered on the railroads. The event's planners expected approximately 500 people, but instead there were over 8,000! From this event, the name "Old Towne Kern" was established and a board of directors was formed to plan further events and stimulate the existing businesses in the area.

Filling Multipurpose Needs

Customers have a finite amount of time each day, so many businesses are developing uniqueness by filling their customers' multiple needs. For example, a California floral shop sends the following note to its customers:

> Dear Friends,
>
> We, at Garden District Flowers are pleased to announce a service to you, our valued customer. We have arranged to give you a unique service that reminds you about special occasions for those you feel especially close to. Please return this letter with the bottom portion filled out, listing those Birthdays, Anniversaries or other occasions you would like a reminder for. We will send you a personal letter at least a week before. In addition, we will provide suggestions for your approval, create that special arrangement, deliver it on time, and add the charge to your account or credit card—all without your having to leave the comfort of your home or office.

Years ago, a *Los Angeles Times* headline read, "Xerox to Unveil Multipurpose Office Machine. Technology: The device can copy, fax, scan images and print documents." This is another example of creating uniqueness by offering a multipurpose product or service. In a similar vein, another newspaper advertisement proclaimed: "A New Idea in Supermarkets Is Taking Shape." The ad described how the Vons supermarket had introduced their superstore, promoting, "From now on, you'll be able to satisfy all your shopping needs under a single roof: Pak-Mail Center, Full-Service Floral, Baja Grill, Dairy/Deli, Video Rental."

Raising the Ante

Universal Studios Hollywood raised the ante by turning its ordinary studio tour into a tourist attraction. "We were too structured," says Ron Bension, the head of theme park operations for MCA. "We really are transforming the experience." The studio now takes visitors through the entire set for Jurassic Park, giving them an experience much like that of the characters in the movie.

Another way to raise the ante is to provide a section in your store or catalogue, or additional services or products, that are more quality driven and expensive. A retail dress shop owner set aside a small area of her store for one-of-a-kind knit sweaters and fancy dresses. Many mail-order catalogues devote one section to more upscale products. Lawyers, accountants, and consultants charge a specified fee, but many of them negotiate higher fees—often above $1,000—for one-hour speaking engagements.

Being the Low-Cost Provider

A chain of all-cosmetics and accessories stores, Ultra-Three Stores, developed its first store near Chicago. According to *Drug Store News*, cosmetics sales increased from $831 million in 1980 to close to $2 billion by 1989, while netting among the category's highest margins. Targeting the off-price clothing shopper, founder Dick George says, "There's opportunity in doing what just plain hasn't been done before."[5]

Many discount stores—Kmart, Wal-Mart, Price-Costco, Mc-Frugals, Home Club, and others—developed their uniqueness by being the low-cost provider in their fields. Their uniqueness centers around a warehouse environment, few staff, variety of inventory, and deeply cut prices.

A recent addition is a group of stores called The Incredible

Universe, owned by Tandy Corporation. The 185,000 square-foot store features every product and brand of electronic equipment available. The store is divided into pavilions, each featuring a type of merchandise. Televisions have their own pavilions; so do computers, printers, faxes, appliances, and electronic games. The store is alive with excitement, including featured entertainment of all types, plus cheerleaders, bands, and jugglers. Recent special events on the Incredible Universe stage were a holiday choir, a kids craft fair, a kids-n-computers seminar, and turkey bowling. All attractions rotate weekly. Since opening day, the Sacramento store has played host to over 40,000 people daily.

An entirely different field, today's health maintenance organizations (HMOs) exhibit their uniqueness by promoting health prevention at a lower cost.

Being Flexible

Gail Gelber, vice-president of sales for a computer company based in Scarsdale, New York, has perfected her unique edge: a "try-before-you-buy" approach. "What I do is convince companies to try a system before buying it—and share their risk with me. This program allows the prospect to install and use my computer for an agreed period. The client then either purchases the system in six months or gives back the equipment without penalty. This sharing approach establishes credibility and a platform to develop relationships."

Airline travelers can now use phones right at their seats, with no assistance from flight attendants. There are computer shuttle trains that offer computer hookups and much more legroom than previously.

Many hotels provide business centers where you can work at a computer, make copies, send express packages, and get the latest stock figures.

Using All the Senses

A one-page ad in *The Wall Street Journal* ran as follows:

> Thank you, America, Today, October 3, 1990 marks the official reunification of Germany. We of Mercedes-Benz

wish to express our sincere and lasting gratitude to the American people for their goodwill. Your steadfast support made this day possible.—Mercedes-Benz of North America, Inc.

This statement was emotionally charged, appealing to several of potential customers' senses. Though indirect in its appeal, it nonetheless engages the reader, who may become a customer. Here are some other examples of how successful companies "use all the senses."

Barry Steinberg at East Coast Direct Tire realized very early in his business that he could use the environment of his shop to make it unique from his competitors. The waiting room is extremely clean with current magazines on racks, sporting such titles as *Sports Illustrated, GQ,* and *Vogue.* Coffee is freshly brewed and there are windows into the shop so you can watch technicians work on your car. The sales people wear shirts, ties, and baseball-style jackets with the company logo; the rest of the crew wear dark blue work pants and T-shirts with the company name and slogan.

A Portland, Oregon, tire store specializes in 4-wheel drive tires and other equipment for 4-wheel drive off-the-road vehicles. The store ran a series of commercials showing the owner of a 4-wheel drive sport vehicle making treks across the Cascade Mountains. Viewers see his black $100,000 rugged vehicle with chrome wheels climb what looks like an impossible slope or descend sharply from a mountaintop. The same type of vehicle is on display in the main store, where customers can examine it—and its tires.

A family entertainment center chain in California offers lunch-time diversion: two hours of fun each Thursday for the low price of $12.99, which includes unlimited rounds of miniature golf and use of "thunder road" race cars, and "splash island" bumper boats. Between 11:00 A.M. and 1:00 P.M., the fee also includes a hot dog and a Pepsi.

There are other examples as well. An independent bookstore in Berkeley, California thrives, even though three other bookstores nearby have gone out of business in the last several years. Why? The store is open from 10:00 A.M. to 10:00 P.M. every day, offers a wide selection of new and used books, presents readings by well-known authors two to four times weekly, features a small but recognized rare-book collection, and has a special section for children. If this weren't enough, it also is a local outlet for *The New York Times,* and the store's staff is large and knowledgeable.

A security business in the Central Valley in California converted an old Victorian house into its office. "We wanted customers to get a feel for our products in a surrounding similar to their own home," explains the owner. "One of the most exciting aspects of our office is that it demonstrates how whether it is an alarm system or a central vacuum, the product can be installed in a new or existing home." His wife adds, "We like customers to examine our work—we are real sticklers for quality products installed as cleanly as possible."

Creative Concepts, a specialty advertising company in California and Hawaii, sells a lot of mugs, T-shirts, and other common items. "Your item is only as good as your artwork," says co-owner Kenyon Sills, "You can sell any mug or pin, but the artwork that goes on it makes it unique. You can use the customer's logo in a unique way." At Kenyon's expense, he gets an artist to produce mockup artwork for specific clients.

Stress the Uniqueness of Your Business

Where is your uniqueness? Here are fifteen ideas to think about while looking for your company's uniqueness, or company identity.

1. *Quality products and services.* Develop a fine quality line of products that speak for themselves, that don't fall apart, that keep their luster for years, and whose prices reflect their perceived values.

2. *Products and services that last.* Stress the uniqueness of your product or service as one that lasts a long time. For example, I have had excellent luck with a Timex watch, known for its durability—it lasts a very long time.

When I owned a dress shop, the clothes wore well for years. In fact, many of my customers were tired of wearing their outfits, but they still looked good. It's been over five years since I've owned the store, but past customers tell me they're still wearing clothes from The First Lady.

The best therapists and consultants are those who give their clients the tools to make changes, rather than have their clients become dependent on them. That's the type of word-of-mouth marketing that brings in a steady flow of new customers.

3. *Professionalism.* Use your certifications and degrees to your advantage. After all, you earned them. A safety professional earned a C.S.P. (Certified Safety Professional) and an ARM (Associate in Risk Management). He announces these certifications on his stationery and business cards, and mentions them in articles he writes for local newspapers. Currently he is seen as the number one safety and claims professional in the city.

4. *Experience.* Customers want their problems fixed. There's a perceived value that the more experienced the company, the better it will be able to help them. For example, a vocational rehabilitation company boasts six certified vocational counselors, with over fifty years of combined experience.

5. *Worthwhile risks.* Take a risk, be different. Creating a new category means taking a risk. Schneider Educational Products publishes children's books; its twist is packaging some with finger puppets. The company's unique approach has captured the attention of big distributors and won it an award from the Publishers Marketing Association. Sharon Schneider is not afraid to take risks. Her first was a software consulting firm that grew to $30 million before it was sold to General Electric.

6. *Mix and match possibilities.* Are the parts of your product line interchangeable with others, similar to a vacuum cleaner? For example, the main product works with several different types of nozzles that need to be purchased separately. Your customers do not want to be part of the "generic" crowd; they want to have it personalized. Find a way to mix and match your products or services for specific clients. For example, a medical billing service provides CD-ROMs for storage retrieval from disk or paper files. The service is adding retrieval capacity for microfiche and expanding

its market to other high-intensive paper chasers, such as attorneys, farmers, accountants, and investment specialists.

Marilyn Fendenlander, of Reno, Nevada, started her company, Research West, by doing readership surveys for the local newspaper. She expanded this to service five other newspapers in the West, then she expanded to doing customer-satisfaction surveys for a major grocery chain and toy-preference interviews with children for a national toy company. Says Marilyn, "I've really just scratched the surface; there are a lot more possibilities out there and I intend to explore them all."

7. *Special orders.* This feature could be part of "being flexible." At the dress shop I once owned, over 35 percent of our business was done on special order. We didn't charge the customer freight, but we didn't have to pay to keep inventory on the floor, either. We felt it was a wash, but the service was perceived by the client as extremely valuable. During our "buys" we added the other colors for the garment and would special order different colors for different customers—"just for their skin tones." Bookstores do the same thing. They special-order a book and do not charge you the freight.

So how can you provide special orders for your clients that bring perceived value to the customer even though it may cost you a few extra dollars? The question you really need to ask is: How can you add special services for your clients? The answer lies in deciding on and promoting your uniqueness.

8. *Easy and low-cost returns.* I rarely do business with mail-order companies because of the fear that if I need to return the item, the process will be complicated and time-consuming.

But a mail-order business with easy return labels and accurate tracking and billing systems can differentiate itself from its competitors.

9. *Risk removal.* Take the risk out of buying. A good return policy with no questions asked is one of the best ways to get people to try your products. Magazine and newsletter subscriptions and audiotapes are famous for their no-risk purchase guarantees. They differentiate themselves by their no-risk guarantees and the free gifts they give. If these free gifts are perceived by the reader as valuable, you have a new customer trying your product.

10. *Time, travel, and stress savers.* Many businesses that attempt to fill customers' multiple needs also save customers time, travel,

and stress. This is what customers want and are willing to pay more for. Personally, I cannot put a price on something that saves me time and alleviates my stress.

Rob Shields, a photographer's agent in Bristol, Rhode Island, discovered that photographers doing international business were under a tremendous strain, trying to maintain their business, do all the travel, and also promote themselves. Currently he represents forty photographers worldwide. He frequently sends clients on assignment to London, India, and Hong Kong. He handles the business and travel details, negotiates fees with the companies that want to hire the photographers, collects the fees, and gives the photographers their share. For this service, the photographers pay a fee, or commission. They get to do more of the part of the business they enjoy doing, and recommend Rob to other photographers.

11. *Customization.* Offer specific delivery options, whether you are dealing with products that go directly to retail customers or offering a service like accounting to a particular industry. When I give seminars for companies, I always customize the sessions to fit the needs of the audience. I phone approximately seven to ten participants ahead of time and ask three questions. I then use this information to slant my presentation and later use the feedback from the seminar for case studies. This way each audience can relate to what I'm talking about and I can communicate an understanding of their interests and concerns.

12. *Glamor.* Sleek photography and specialized make-up applications service the uniqueness of your business. A dress store does color analysis on its customers, offering a specialized service to help bring out the unique beauty of each shopper. Interesting note: Dress shops have notoriously not appreciated color analysis because it has narrowed the customer's choices rather than given more ideas on colors. In a similar vein, our company works with a photographer who has separate prices for regular pictures and for the more sophisticated pictures that are used in brochures, from oilfield shots to aerial photos.

13. *Customer Interaction.* Become interactive with your customer. On the back side of Tom's of Maine toothpaste it reads, "Dear Friends and New Customers, . . . Try it and let us know what you think. Your Friends, Tom and Kate."

14. *Accessibility.* Make it easy for the customer to speak or write to the CEO or president of the company, the author of a book, or the "guru" in your specific field of interest. Harvey McKay, author of *Swim with the Sharks* and owner of an envelope company, returns many of the calls he receives and writes to other readers whom he cannot call back.

On the back page of my first book, *Where Did The Time Go?* I encouraged readers to contact me by phone (collect call since I do not have a national 800 number) or write directly to me.

15. *Real customer service.* Don't just offer lip service. Examples such as Barry Steinberg at East Coast Direct Tire, Nordstrom's Department Stores, and successful others give real service, not lip service.

Susan Abrams is a bed and breakfast reservationist who says she really has two types of customers to satisfy, and she gives both superior service or she's out of business. First, her bed & breakfast reservation service handles forty-three establishments in South Carolina. These establishments are her customers, but so are the people who call in for reservations.[5]

TIME TIP: Conduct three different brainstorming sessions: one with your employees (if you have no employees, then with the people you outsource with); one with your suppliers, vendors, or distributors; and one with your clients. Ask the following five questions in each session:

1. *How do you see what we do as different from our competitors?*
2. *What do you see as our strengths? Our weaknesses?*
3. *How could we better serve you?*
4. *How can we bring more perceived value in our product or service?*
5. *Are there any other changes you suggest?*

Using this type of brainstorming session saves time in the long run and gives you perspectives that would be difficult to reach on your own.

The Uniqueness Formula

Personalizing your product or service, developing a company identity, and producing perceived value by your customer will provide you with a uniqueness for your business. The formula is:

$$\text{Personalization} + \text{company identity} + \\ \text{perceived value} = \text{Uniqueness}$$

Summary

Companies that develop products, programs, and services to promote the customer's feeling of being unique will be the most successful. Personalizing your services and products will provide higher profits for your business.

Six ways to create uniqueness in your business are: recreating something that has been lost or restoring a memory, filling multipurpose needs, raising the ante, being the low-cost provider, being flexible, and using all the senses.

Where is your company uniqueness? You may want to consider the fifteen ideas given in the chapter for finding your unique edge: (1) quality products and services, (2) products and services that last, (3) professionalism, (4) experience, (5) worthwhile risks, (6) mix and match possibilities, (7) special orders, (8) easy and low-cost returns, (9) risk removal, (10) time, travel, and stress savers, (11) customization, (12) glamor, (13) customer interaction, (14) accessibility, and (15) real customer service.

You can find your company's uniqueness by asking your staff, your vendors and suppliers, and your customers what sets you apart from the competition. The uniqueness formula states that personalization plus company identity plus perceived value equals uniqueness, thereby increasing cash flow and profits.

Notes

1. Faith Popcorn, *The Popcorn Report* (New York: Bantam Doubleday Dell, 1991). Copyright © 1991 by Faith Popcorn. Used by permission of Doubleday, a division of Bantam Doubleday Dell Publishing Group, Inc.

2. Ibid.
3. William R. "Max" Carey, Jr., "The New You," *Inc.* magazine, August 1991.
4. Ibid.
5. Leslie Brokaw, "Team Make-Up," *Inc.* magazine, September 1990, p. 27. Reprinted with permission, *Inc.* magazine, September 1990. Copyright © 1990 by Goldhirsh Group, Inc., 38 Commercial Wharf, Boston, Massachusetts 02110.

5

Dealing With the Media

Every business can create a tremendous amount of free publicity with the expenditure of a relatively few marketing dollars and not much time. News releases of expansions, specialty activities, and awards attract the attention of editors and reporters. Press kits sent to the media ahead of a planned event generate attendance at press conferences and advance publicity. And finally, a business person can create easy access to the reader by becoming an authoritative source for the press. For example, a veterinarian might let the press know that he or she is available to answer questions about pets or might start a pet column for a local newspaper. An accountant can become an expert on the local economy; a dress shop operator can become a fashion expert; a music store owner, the local jazz expert; and a candy store manager can provide decorating ideas and dessert recipes for weddings, anniversaries, and other events.

The "Whys" and "Hows" of Free Publicity

Advertising and publicity are different. You pay for radio, television, or print advertisements. Advertisements are used for receiving an instant response to a new product or service, or in developing and maintaining brand identity over the long run. Publicity, however, is free promotion about you, your product, or your service. Articles, feature stories, quotes, and interviews make up the bulk of this free publicity.

Publicity creates the perception of credibility. An article written about you and your business, or your being interviewed on television or radio, is much more believable to the average person than a purchased advertisement. Advertising has its place, but only as reinforcement to your marketing plan, not in place of it.

Publicity is free, credible, and far-reaching. Friends and clients may comment on the article written about you and your business, even though it appeared five months earlier. Publicity has an enduring quality. Of course, negative publicity can remain with a person or company for many months or years. But the same is true for positive publicity, which is what you are looking for.

Publicity Ideas by the Dozen

Here are twelve ways to get the attention of the media.

Be Persistent

One publicity article is not enough. People need to repeatedly hear, see, or talk about your service or product for you to see results. It is estimated that it takes customers six to eight times of hearing, seeing, or talking about your company before they buy or break their habit of buying your competitor's services or products.

"I spent one full year getting national publicity for my concerts, books, and albums. I spent over five hours a day doing my own publicity, calling and sending information," says Tanja Evetts Weimer, national motivational speaker and entertainer. But, she adds, "this year I am completely filled with speaking dates."

Time Tip: Plan your publicity calendar approximately three months in advance. This forces you to focus on what you want publicized—for example, a new product, additional benefits of an existing product or service, tie-in with national media, or a new position on a board—and allow enough time to generate interest.

Take a Long-Range View

The media are busy with deadlines and other people pitching their stories, and your news tip may not always get immediate attention. So try other ways to get people's attention, which may ultimately net you publicity. In my experience, there are more cooperative media people than not. This is especially true of high-level personnel—producers, directors, or editors. If you can make their life easier, they are all ears.

For example, call a television producer and ask what the upcoming talk shows are planning to air, then offer ideas on how you can help. Refer to other people you feel could help them, too. In the process, you will have developed a relationship with the producer, even though you weren't interviewed "this time around."

I keep a file of people who interview my clients or myself for radio, television, or print. I periodically call them to see how I may be of help to them in finding a source for something they are working on. When they are working on a project that utilizes my skills or my client's skills, I get a call and many times a quote.

Eva Friederichs, owner of Images of Success Esthetic Institute, gave a seminar to estheticians in Philadelphia. To publicize the seminar, I called nine media contacts, sent press releases, followed up, and one television station made plans to interview her. As a result of the interview, the station received 190 calls within the next four hours. Later in this chapter I include a copy of the actual press release that was sent.

TIME TIP: *Organization is the key when making media contacts. Write the names of your media contacts on 3 × 5 cards with the following information: name of contact, phone number, type of medium, date of initial contact, date material is sent, dates of follow-up calls. The 3 × 5 card for the Philadelphia contact looks like this:*

```
        Trudy Haynes          Television
        Philadelphia, Pa      Phone number
```

- contacted August 15—wants a media kit
- sent media kit August 18
- followed up on media kit August 22
- followed up to say ''hi'' and plan an interview time—August 25
- followed up in writing on designated time—September 2
- followed up after show to see how things went
- sent three more containers of product to Trudy

Over the years I learned to keep simple and clear notes of phone calls and mailings. Records kept on 3 × 5 cards are easy to maintain, so you stay organized and achieve a greater success rate of media acceptance and exposure.

Nurture Your Media Relationships

There are specific ways to develop these media relationships. Write a thank-you note to your contact, even when that person has said "No, thank you." The producer may not need your information this time around, but the thank-you serves two purposes: It thanks the person for his or her time and help, and it gives the producer another chance to remember who you are. Thank-you notes are remembered. Fran Halpern, who hosts a weekly television show in Santa Barbara, California, says, "I remember every thank-you card I've received, because there haven't been that many."

TIME TIP: *It takes only a few minutes to write a thank-you note and the chances are good that it will open the door for you in the future.*

Do Not Become Self-Serving

Media people are interested in reporting the news, lifestyle points of interests, new technology, major or emerging trends, controversial topics, medical trends, and dozens of other topics. The bottom line is that you must "pitch" your ideas in ways that the media's audiences will find interesting.

Most small businesses can't understand why the local paper won't cover their open house, business anniversary, or other "business" events. Unless you find a way to present that open house as real news or tie it in to a charity function, a community service, or some other event, the media will not cover it and rightfully so. Publicity is available for promoting new ideas and new products, not to sell your inventory.

A temporary personnel agency prepared for its open house at its new location and called the press. "They just weren't interested in covering our open house in our new office site. I thought that they cover local business," said Jason Mahoney, the company's co-owner. So instead, we developed a charity tie-in program for the personnel agency, showing how a percentage of the profits from the agency would be presented by check on the night of the open house. Both a television station and a newspaper covered the event.

Time Tip: With a little preplanning, you can combine a business event and add on a non self-serving tie-in; a certain percentage of the proceeds of the event goes to a charity; you call a press conference before the event and give the media new trends in your industry; develop a survey and announce the results at the event.

Remember to give the media information, facts, and statistics that will be well received by their audience. A little planning goes a long way in gaining visibility for your company.

Create a Media Mix

A media mix of publicity includes radio, television, cable, magazines, weekly circulars, newspapers, trade journals, newsletters, and any other media communications. A media mix provides consistent coverage through a variety of channels and allows television watchers, radio listeners, and readers to all know you and your company. Promoting your business with a mix of communications adds energy to your publicity campaign by reaching more people.

Time Tip: Initially finding your contacts takes the most time. However, once you know whom to contact and have developed a media relationship with those people, your publicity "time" is the time it takes to make a phone call or two.

Keep Your Eyes and Ears Open

Stay tuned to what is happening locally, nationally, and internationally. A startup company wanted national publicity for a new food product and its entrepreneur membership club. After a national election that swung the country to the right, the company linked that conservative trend to its new entrepreneurial club.

Newspapers and magazines carried articles about the club's founders, bringing attention to the new business.

TIME TIP: Read at least one newspaper daily and a current events magazine weekly to follow trends and happenings. Keep your antennae up and contact any media personnel who could use your expertise.

Follow Up

Regular and persistent follow-up is essential for receiving the benefits of the media. Because of deadlines and the sheer volume of information they receive, media people often need a friendly reminder. The business editor forgot about our initial conversation and could not find the media kit I sent. Three days after he received the second packet, I followed up with a second call. I did this with great success: My client was booked for an interview during lunch!

TIME TIP: By referring to your handy 3 × 5 cards, you can quickly identify which media representatives will respond to your press release.

Keep a Media Database

Start a media file that includes the names of all the contacts you make, whether successful or not. Make separate categories for television, radio, newspapers, newsletters, and magazines. This way you can easily add new names and replace others when they switch positions.

TIME TIP: Send your media contacts Christmas cards and company newsletters—the same material you send your customers.

Use the Phone Book as a Research Tool

The phone book is a great resource. George Martin, whose law firm sponsors a business conference that attracts the attention of national media says, "I use the phone book for finding speakers and vendors for the conference." Chuck Guy, vice-president of marketing for an international manufacturing company, commented at a local American Marketing Association meeting that "you need to use the telephone book to find the companies you want to work with. It's easy and saves time."

TIME TIP: I use the **World Chamber of Commerce Directory** *and call local chambers of commerce for the phone numbers of television and radio stations as well as the print media in that particular city. I also go to the library and look through the yellow pages of that city for listings of the local media. To obtain a copy of the* **World Chamber of Commerce Directory,** *write:*

World Chamber of Commerce Directory
P.O. Box 1029
Loveland, CO 80539
(303) 663-3231; fax (303) 663-6187

Be Active in Civic Organizations and Attend Conferences

An excellent avenue for free publicity is active participation in civic organizations: chambers of commerce, men's and women's clubs, and trade organizations in your field. Volunteer to chair a fundraiser or conference. Becoming a spokesperson for these groups will bring publicity for the event and credibility to you and your business at the same time. Todd Hansen, salesperson for an outside billboard company, arrived in a new city in a new state over eighteen months ago. "I volunteered to take over the Ad Club. We were getting around fourteen people in attendance every month, and now after the membership drive we have over four hundred members with one hundred active ones." I saw Todd's name in newspaper clippings and in organization newsletters, which prompted me to call him to be a team captain for the chamber of commerce's membership drive. It would be an occasion for more free publicity and the opportunity to meet new people.

TIME TIP: Choose only two or three organizations and become active in each. You may want to add one new organization a year, but cancel membership in an earlier one. This rotation of dropping one organization and adding a new one allows you to meet new people, become active in other organizations, and have an opportunity to learn new skills.

Target Your Mailings

Find specific media contacts and send your materials directly to them. Sending out unlimited press releases to media fax numbers or addresses is a time waster and not a successful way to approach publicity. Take the time to find out the names of the appropriate people and send your materials to their attention.

TIME TIP: Call your media contacts first to see if they are interested in your information. Most media people prefer an initial phone call to check their interest and their calendar.

Ask for Referrals

If your local television station doesn't cover your area of publicity, ask which ones do. If your newspaper contact is not interested or does not cover your type of information, ask for a suggestion as to who does. There is no competition or one-upsmanship likely to arise if your contact is not interested in your publicity idea and does not cover this type of business.

TIME TIP: You don't want to reinvent the wheel. Take advantage of the expertise and experience of others by asking questions. Most people want to help. And don't forget to write a thank-you note.

Creating Effortless News Releases

The press release is a primary means by which you can get the attention of the media. But to get their attention, your press release must stand out from the hundreds of other releases that the print and electronic media receive each day. Always answer the following questions when developing your press release: Who? What? When? Where? Why? You need to write a release with an angle that reaches those viewers or readers who "care" about the information presented. Answering this question helps prevent your press release from becoming self-serving.

Press releases *do* get results. My client was interviewed by several national and international newspapers, magazines, and newsletters. And the response from a media contact who had received her press kit was as follows. The *Inspirator International* is the Pacific-Rim's largest circulation English-language magazine serving personal motivation, self-help, management and sales training, inspirational guidance, and human development.

The results of this client's press release are as follows:

Dear Ms. Klein:

Thank you very much for your recent envelope. You accomplished an outstanding job of presenting your client to us.

Based on your presentation, we would like to do a large-space feature article on her, presenting her as an international role model among motivators and sales trainers.

Could you please forward this letter on to your client as I would like to begin a dialogue with her about the article.

Possibly we can get a full-color cover pix (of her) on the planned feature, if we can create a piece that does her justice.

Again, thank you, and please put us in touch with your client.

Sincerely,
Forrest W. Cato
USA Editor
The Inspirator International

Here is an example of the actual press release and the ensuing results:

Eva Friederichs, Founder and President of Images of Success Esthetic Institute, will be in Philadelphia, Pa., September 13 through 17 (available for interviews in the afternoons), to speak on skin-care products that reverse aging and skin analysis on different types of skin.

Eva Friederichs: Eva started her career in Philadelphia nearly 30 years ago. She is the Founder and President of the first advanced training facility for estheticians in the U.S. The industry magazine *Dermascope* refers to her as a legend. She is involved in skin care, cosmetics, nutrition, and body care.

Eight years ago, Friederichs introduced her namesake skincare line, Natural Skin Care by Eva, followed by Color Images Enhancers by Eva, an upscale cosmetics line, Essential Oils by Eva, and Body Images by Eva.

Currently, Eva products are sold in over 2,000 salons, resorts, and health spas throughout the U.S. and are now available through mail order.

Friederichs holds a CIDESCO Diploma, the only international certificate available in the U.S., and is a strong supporter of women entrepreneurs.

She was a finalist for Woman Entrepreneur of the Year from NAWBO (National Association of Women Business Owners).

Eva is also working in the field of facial trauma, age spots, and scarring.

Contact Eva Friederichs at
[phone number listings]
Available mornings for interviews;
early mornings are the best times to call.

What were the results of this press release? Eva was interviewed on a television talk show and received 190 calls within four hours; Trudy Haynes, the TV host, commented on the products the next day and Eva's company received 150 calls. One week later, Trudy mentioned the products for a third time and Eva received 91 additional calls. Eva has also been interviewed for several newspapers, national magazines, and newsletters.

Samson Johns Associates, a public relations firm in Omaha, Nebraska, began sending its own news releases on its own business and clients' progress directly to prospective clients. Today, the releases are the company's top generator of new business leads, bringing annual sales in excess of $20 million.

Every month the company sends out an announcement of a new account, awards it has won, or new personnel it has hired to 100 members of the press, 150 clients, and 500-plus prospective clients. What results does this action have? One to five new prospects call to learn more about the company. "Resist the urge to turn a news release into a sales pitch," senior vice-president James Pitcher says, "or the release will alienate the press and won't impress prospects. People say they read about us in the paper. Nine times out of ten I bet they are remembering the press release."

Here are seven tips for increasing the effectiveness of your press or news releases:

1. *Keep it neat.* The best press releases are clean and easy to read. Media people work under deadlines. If the release is difficult to read, they will throw it away. Use white paper. Colored paper, when faxed, is difficult to read.
2. *Make it typewritten, double-spaced.* The more space on one page, the easier it is to read and make notes. Typing the release is another way to keep it neat and easy to read.
3. *Keep it to one or two pages.* Always think of time savings for your media contact. If the release can't be written in one or two pages maximum, you're not getting to the heart of the issue.
4. *Keep it accurate.* One of the best ways to develop a relationship with the media is to present accurate information, not fluff. The fluff may be accepted once, but probably not again. If our company does not find an angle that will work in a press release, we go back to brainstorming.
5. *Make four critical points of information prominent: The contact person, contact phone number, best time to reach contact person, and availability of dates and times to be interviewed should stand out on the page.*
6. *Follow up with a call.* Check to see if everyone received the information you sent. With good intentions but busy schedules, media personnel need to be reminded of the releases they've received. If you're providing information that will

be of interest to their readers and viewers, you will feel comfortable following up.

7. *Send a thank-you note.* Always send a note of gratitude, even if your press release is not picked up *this time.* The thank-you note keeps the dialogue open for your next approach. I sent a freelance writer a thank-you note after she turned down an idea I had presented. Within two months, she called me for information for an article she was writing!

The ABCs of a Good Press Kit

Be sure to include all of the following in the press kits you send out to media representatives.

☐ Black and white picture of yourself, professionally photographed.

☐ A one-page compact biography of yourself, your skills, and your accomplishments.

☐ Copies of any articles written about you or by you.

☐ A one- or two-page press release.

☐ Video segments of previous television interviews.

☐ Audiotapes of previous radio interviews.

☐ Any timely stories or controversial data appropriate to sell your idea.

☐ Samples of your product or testimonials of your service.

Becoming a Media Expert

You should become familiar with the titles of people who work in the media and whom you should ask to speak to when you want to get publicity.

Producer (Radio/TV): Usually the person responsible for booking you on a talk show or to be interviewed by phone.

Associate Producer (Radio/TV):	In a large organization, several people are responsible for booking appearances. In fact, one associate producer is responsible for lifestyle, another for business, and another for food and travel.
News Director (Radio/TV):	Usually the person to whom to pitch your news story.
Program Director or Manager (Radio/TV):	The person responsible for coordinating guests and all other programming.
Executive Producer (Radio/TV):	The key person responsible for who ultimately gets on the show.
Editor or Associate Editor (Print):	Usually responsible for specific areas of coverage; features and lifestyle, book reviews, celebrity mentions, news, and others.

Media Contacts for You to Use

The following are some of the network television and radio programs and nationwide magazines that are receptive to publicity suggestions.

Television:

"20/20"
ABC News
147 Columbus Avenue
New York, NY 10023
(212) 456-2020
(212) 456-2969 fax

"60 Minutes"
CBS News
555 West 57th Street
New York, NY 10019
(212) 975-2831
(212) 757-6975

"CBS This Morning"
CBS News
524 West 57th Street, Suite 44
New York, NY 10019
(212) 975-6407
(212) 975-2115 fax

"Donahue"
30 Rockefeller Plaza, Suite 827
New York, NY 10112
(212) 664-6501
(212) 757-5386 fax

"Good Morning America"
ABC News
147 Columbus Avenue, 6th
   Floor
New York, NY 10023
(212) 456-5900
(212) 456-5962 fax

"Live with Regis and Kathie
   Lee"
WABC-TV
7 Lincoln Square, 5th Floor
New York, NY 10023
(212) 456-3054
(212) 496-5249 fax

Magazines:

Better Homes and Gardens
1716 Locust Street
Des Moines, IA 50309-3023
(515) 284-2336
(515) 284-3684 fax

First for Women
270 Sylvan Avenue
Englewood Cliffs, NJ 07632
(201) 569-6699
(201) 569-6264 fax

Good Housekeeping
959 8th Avenue
New York, NY 10019
(212) 649-2280
(212) 265-3307 fax

Life Magazine
Time-Life Bldg., Rockefeller
   Center
New York, NY 10020
(212) 522-1212
(212) 522-0379

Modern Maturity
3200 East Carson Street
Lakewood, CA 90712
(310) 496-2277
(310) 496-4124 fax

Money
Time-Life Bldg., Rockefeller
   Center
New York, NY 10020
(212) 522-1212
(212) 522-0189 fax

Newsweek
444 Madison Avenue
New York, NY 10022
(212) 350-4000
(212) 350-4120 fax

People
Time-Life Bldg., Rockefeller
   Center
New York, NY 10020
(212) 522-1212
(212) 522-0884 fax

Summary

Sending press kits to the media ahead of a planned event or an announcement generates free publicity for you and your business. Publicity is free, credible, far-reaching, and long-lasting promotion for the people who choose to use it.

Twelve suggestions for effective press contacts are: (1) being persistent; (2) taking a long-range view; (3) nurturing your media relationships; (4) not becoming self-serving; (5) creating a media mix; (6) keeping your eyes and ears open; (7) following up; (8) keeping a media database; (9) using the phone book as a research tool; (10) being active in civic organizations and attending conferences; (11) targeting your mailings; (12) asking for referrals.

Think of the media as your partner in growing your business and keep them informed of what you're doing.

6

Humor:
A Serious Customer
Marketing Tool

More and more businesses use humor as both an internal and an external customer marketing tool. C. W. Metcalf, a humor consultant in Fort Collins, Colorado, has made a business of creating a better business climate and reducing business stress through the use of humor.

Allen Klein, humor educator and self-proclaimed "Jollytologist," says "Laughter gives your heart and lungs a deep-breathing workout comparable to that of aerobic exercise."[1] Research shows that physiologically when you laugh, almost every part of your body is affected and your heart rate and blood pressure go up. Dr. William Fry, Jr., suggests that three minutes of genuine belly laughter is equal to twenty minutes of rowing exercise. It's similar to internal jogging—even the respiratory system gets a work-out when heavy laughter brings about coughing.

Humor as a Healthy Coping Skill

It is difficult to maintain muscle tension when you are laughing hard. Have you ever laughed so hard that you were doubled over, your stomach started hurting, you spit up your food, or you wet your pants? Humor brings about laughter and laughter brings about a biochemical change. Several medical studies have shown that a sense of humor makes people healthier and helps defend them against illness by reducing stress.

"Men talk about killing the competition. Once you start think-ing like that, you can die of business," humor consultant Metcalf says. "That's what terminal professionalism is about. They know you're serious about your work when you get a heart attack, a bleeding ulcer, or a divorce." This may be because researchers have found that a naturally produced drug, cortisol, is released when people laugh. Cortisol is an immune suppressor.

So how does this translate to you and your business? Exter-nally, companies use a great deal of humor in their ads and direct mail pieces. Internally, they use humor to help employees deal with both customers and other people in the company. Your effort can be as simple as using an in-store cartoon bulletin board, or as extensive as creating a complete humorous image extending through your logo, advertising, and in-store atmosphere.

In short, humor in business can go a long way. For example, humor fosters creative brainstorming, inspires marketing cam-paigns, promotes a positive attitude and business image, disarms sexism within the company, boosts employee morale, and eases personal tension.

Humor Fosters Creative Brainstorming

Studies show that employees who have fun at work are more cre-ative and productive. Humor leads you to create funny stories, fan-tasies, take-offs of television shows, amusing headlines, plays on politics, and other material to lighten the atmosphere and inspire the creation of new ideas.

Dr. Bob Maurer, a psychiatrist, says "that most people look for ideas in creative places, but creative people look for ideas and input in ordinary and unlikely places."[2] For example, a successful trial attorney calls in the office janitors to listen to his jury summa-tions. If they understand it, then he knows the jurors will. Dr. Maurer goes on to say, "The screenwriter for the movie *Nine to Five* flew to Cleveland and asked secretaries about their jobs. He also asked the secretaries if they ever thought about killing their bosses. He had overwhelming responses and a movie was born." Clearly, the screenwriter saw the creative potential in a humorous situation, one that was common to many businesses.

Fear and creativity go hand in hand. "The greater the amount of fear, the more the body's natural impulses bypass the thinking process and we revert to old doubts and critical messages we received as children," states Maurer. Humor helps alleviate those fears, or at least put them into perspective. Once in perspective, the ideas begin to flow, as in brainstorming.

Dr. Maurer suggests the following ideas on creatively brainstorming:[3]

- Ideally, put people in different fields or walks of life together in a session.
- Dismiss no idea initially.
- Use a facilitator who can keep people aware of the rules.
- Be sure participants focus on the problem and know why they're attending the session.
- Write down and file discarded ideas.
- Have fun with the process and don't be interested in the immediate results.

"Ironically, the end results of a brainstorming session are the best when everyone isn't focused on it," states Dr. Maurer. "Collaboration is harder to do than recognized because we're so competitive. It's truly hard." By lightening up the atmosphere, ultimately you'll get better results.

Humor Sells Products and Services

For years Avis was the number two car rental business, but the company made the most of it—using humor. Its slogan, "We try harder" became famous. Likewise, an advertisement for CNBC, the business-talk cable network, is using humor to keep viewers watching. One ad shows a woman in a conversation about gun control. She thought gun control would be much stricter after the shooting of JR (the 1980s television show "Dallas"). Funny? Yes, it is humor at work, making a point because it makes an impression on the viewers.

I see ads and the question asked is "Why does the world get so serious when you grow up? Aren't there still strawberries to be stolen? Lakes to skinny dip in? Cigars to smoke? When exercised regularly, your funny bone's the last to go." They may be jokes, but people remember the product, too.

With a total investment of $12,000 in 1978, Ben Cohen and Jerry Greenfield opened up their first homemade ice cream parlor in an abandoned gas station in Burlington, Vermont. Today, Ben & Jerry's has annual sales of over $100 million. Their unofficial motto is, "If it's not fun, why do it?" Ben & Jerry's built a multi-million dollar business using two driving forces: a social conscience and a sense of humor.

Humor Promotes a Positive Attitude and a Positive Business Image

You can use humor to suggest that your company has a positive attitude and a positive business image. The Alternative Copy Shop in Santa Barbara, California, uses humor in its name. Years ago, in a college community, a restaurant called The Hip Bagel used humor by serving only hamburgers on its bagels.

Another Example of Humor Creating a Positive Attitude

A stockbrokerage firm in Portland, Oregon, sends out stickers on monthly correspondence with funny messages, "because stock prices and dividends can be humorous," comments Rick Davis, a high volume stockbroker.

Humor Disarms Sexism

Women often use humor to downplay sexist remarks and discourage sexual "come-ons." Jennifer Stone, a family attorney in Witchita, Kansas, works with newly divorced women and men. Many of these men would like to date her. "I feel badly to flatly reject them, since people coming out of a divorce have their fill of rejection—I just make light of their comments and advances and we laugh together. This type of humor keeps the relationship professional."

Leslie Sullenger, a life insurance agent, recently chatted with a potential client who made the comment, "That's something a female would say." She responded by saying, "What would the other half of the population say?" "I think my comment caught him by surprise and he started to laugh." Humor worked here as a first resource. When in doubt, use humor first.

Humor Boosts Employee Morale

Adia, with headquarters in Redwood City, California, is a personnel placement service organization. The company surveyed 1,160 human resource professionals, who shared information on how their businesses use humor to keep up morale and relieve job stress. The results are as follows:[4]

> 77 percent tell a joke to break the ice at a staff meeting.
> 75 percent encourage employees to display humorous cartoon or comic strips.
> 52 percent use humor to lighten deadline pressure.
> 39 percent promote "laugh breaks" among their employees.
> 50 percent think hiring a "humor consultant" to train employees to lighten up is a viable idea.

A telecommunications company has weekly "mirth meetings." "We all bring in cartoons or funny customer stories at the meetings," says Daniel Wallace, general manager. "The funny stories are remembered and the humor allows for dynamic discussions."

One of the nation's leading discounters, Sam Walton, founder of Wal-Mart Stores, gave his employees a challenge: If the employees could "achieve the impossible" by producing record profits for the fiscal year, he would then dance the hula down Wall Street. The employees "achieved the impossible" and Sam Walton danced in a grass skirt down the main street of the country's financial center.

"There's something about seeing a college photo of your CEO wearing tie-dyed pants and love beads that's good for morale," says Malcolm Kushner, a former attorney who now is a humor consultant. "Humor sanctioned by management sends the message that this place is okay. They don't mind if you have fun. It also works to the company's benefit in the public arena."

So ask your employees to write down seven things they enjoy doing that makes them laugh and the approximate time they last did them. Your employees will be surprised to see how infrequently they allow themselves to participate in activities they enjoy doing. Through the use of humor in the workplace, you can show them that fun times occur during work hours as well.

How to Use Humor as a Business Tool

Dr. Barbara Mackoff, author and nationally prominent consultant in business and psychology, offers four keys to using humor as a professional tool:[5]

1. Direct your humor to the situation, not the person. Try to avoid the Don Rickles sarcasm and blame.
2. Focus laughter on the problem, not on yourself. You want to stay away from blaming and poking fun at yourself. It is much better to poke fun at the situation.
3. Use Mackoff's M-B-A formula: Mirror—make fun of the situation by playing with the image at hand; Borrow—create comic relief by comic comparison (Mackoff's example is "This year's budget is a kind of Zen experience—we now find ourselves contemplating nothingness . . ."); and Anticipate—use humor to anticipate resistance or defensiveness from colleagues or clients ("I'm just calling for the tenth time today"; or "Have you had your aggravation yet for today?")
4. Cultivate humor as a state of mind. Enjoy "silent comedy" to create in your mind a comic image that removes you from the stress of the moment. Mackoff suggests that, in the middle of a frustrating period, "picture yourself in the candy factory episode of 'I Love Lucy' where Lucy and Ethel tried to keep up with the candy rolling down the high-speed assembly line," says Mackoff.

You can insert humor almost anywhere, anytime in business. The following are a few ideas for you to use:

- Send funny cards to clients as a thank-you.
- Send humorous cards to clients during or after a stressful situation.

- Keep a "humor" bulletin board in the kitchen or coffee area where employees are encouraged to put up cartoons, funny pictures, and so on.
- Start meetings with five to ten minutes of "funny" client stories.
- Pass cartoons around the office during mid-week for no reason, "just because."
- Send a funny card whenever someone at work is going through a difficult personal transition.
- Even if you don't feel you can tell jokes, you can present humorous personal anecdotes at a speech.

But there's one cardinal rule to remember: Don't use sarcasm or insults for a laugh!

Tickling Your Customer's Funny Bone

You can achieve positive results in your business in myriad ways. For example, a retail store sends a different joke every month with the customer's statement. The store claims that this idea started as fun, but it finds customers pay their invoices earlier. In the same way, a bank in Palo Alto, California, has a sense of humor. Once a year it purchases 15,000 pounds of onions and hands them out to its customers, with the motto: "No-tears banking."

At Southwest Airlines, employees are encouraged to make paper airplanes from old memos. The company has the best on-time performance and fewer customer complaints than most other airlines. Part of both Levi Strauss and Dreyer's Ice Cream companies' mission statements is "to have fun in their work."

Will all this humor put customers off? No. Allen Klein, the jollytologist, says that "you can be professional and have a good time."[6] In Klein's book, *The Healing Power of Humor*, he explains that humor is appropriate almost any time, including in such stressful places as hospitals. Allen works with hospital staff to show them how to lighten up and decrease their stress levels. He suggests that if you send someone a memo and the person loses it, then "send a memo 2 feet by 3 feet." That gets your point across, but in a humorous way.

Allen offers six ideas to add humor to your life, both at home and at work:

1. Exaggerate situations to find the humor in them. "Look at cartoonists; they take everyday situations and exaggerate," says Klein. One exercise he uses with his audiences is to take the hands off the clock and replace them with the numbers thirteen through fifteen. Time certainly looks differently then.
2. Use props. Allen uses props wherever he goes. "I have a clown nose, a smile mask, a pickle that whistles. Props are reminders to lighten up."
3. Have a "Ha-Ha" bulletin board. "Humor is a bonding element," says Allen.
4. Put cartoons in paychecks. "Most paychecks are jokes anyway," says Klein.
5. Find a humor buddy.
6. Dress up your desk with something that will make you laugh or feel good. Keep a picture of your giggling friends, children, or staff on your desk.

Says Allen Klein, "If I could, I would have a feather in my book to help lighten things up."[7]

Create a Client-Humor

Keep records of your humorous contacts with clients. Start a client-humor time line, listing your clients and the dates you send them "humorous" information. This way you'll keep in contact with your clients and maintain strong, healthy, and loyal relationships.

The client-humor time line looks like this:

Client	Date Sent	Humor Description

Check your humor time line frequently and repeat your contacts quarterly. If you send quarterly newsletters to your clients, add a humor section with jokes, anecdotes, and other related humorous stories.

Summary

Humor in business can go a long way. It fosters creative brainstorming, effective marketing campaigns, a positive attitude and business image; it disarms sexism, boosts employee morale, and eases personal tension. Fear and creativity go hand in hand. The more fear and demands placed on a person, the less creative that person becomes as an employee.

Some fun ways to keep your mind and environment lighthearted are to send funny cards to clients, maintain a humor bulletin board in the kitchen or coffee area, start meetings with humorous client stories, pass cartoons around the office "just because," exaggerate the stressful situation to see the humor in it, and keep something humorous on your desk. Never use sarcasm or insults to get a laugh. In short, humor relieves stress and creates a productive and creative atmosphere.

Notes

1. Allen Klein, *The Healing Power of Humor* (New York: Putnam, 1989).
2. Bob Maurer, psychologist; interview, Les Kelley Family Health Center, Santa Monica, California.
3. Ibid.
4. Adia, Redwood City, California.
5. Barbara Mackoff, "Humor as a Professional Tool," *Executive Female*, November/December 1990, p. 57.
6. Klein, op. cit., and personal interview.
7. Ibid.

7

Creative Marketing

A company can double and triple its business simply by applying creativity to its marketing. A dress shop created a stir by treating its customers to an in-store breakfast fashion show. A small auto-parts shop turned the industry upside down by providing customers with a 24-hour phone line, so night owls had access to both information and parts around the clock. A plumber painted the picture of a bare foot on his truck and invited customers to call the "barefoot" plumber. This chapter helps businesses unlock their marketing creativity and offers dozens of suggestions for putting excitement and pizazz into their every operation.

A Note About Creativity

It is my opinion that everyone is creative. Whether people choose to use this creativity or not is another matter. And I see creativity as thinking about doing things in new ways or developing new products while keeping the needs of the customer in the forefront. As an example, let's look at that in-store breakfast fashion show as it applies to creative marketing.

The owner of a sportswear shop liked using her customers to model because it was a way to get them into the store at no risk to the customer. And the customers were flattered at being asked to model. However, great care went into each model's dress selections, and with a store discount for modeling, most women bought at least one outfit of the three or four they wore.

The breakfast fashion shows started before the store opened, at 8:30 A.M., and lasted until 10:00 A.M. to allow quality time for the presentation. Invitations for the breakfast went to customers, and were followed up with a phone call.

Breakfast usually consisted of spinach quiche, orange juice, fresh fruit, muffins, and coffee. Quite often, customers would ask for the quiche recipe. In one and a half hours, over $1,000 in merchandise was sold and leftover food was available for customers after the store opened. The store was in such disarray, with clothes, jewelry, and belts scattered around, that it caused a certain "excitement" when regular customers came in. These monthly breakfast fashion shows netted the business two to three good days of sales. In short, a little creativity went a long way toward building customer satisfaction and increasing the cash flow.

Never Say No to a Customer

A large part of creative marketing centers around the word *no.* Let's look at six reasons why you don't want to say no to customers.

1. *Talk to your client.* If a client wants a service or a certain product that you don't have or have provided only in the past, ask the individual what he or she is going to use the product for or why it is needed. Once you know what the need is to be resolved, you can direct the person to something similar that will give the same result.

Creative marketing: Suggest alternative ways of doing something that may be less costly, take less time, or have any number of other angles. If you say no right off the bat, you have lost the customer's interest and possibly a sale.

2. *Stay positive.* When people hear the word *no,* they get an empty, negative feeling, even though they may not be conscious of this subtle internal reaction. It's all part of our conditioning during childhood.

Creative marketing: Keep the transaction positive. You don't want to create a negative feeling, thought, or word in your communications. "No" puts your relationship with the client or customer at a "minus." You'll have to work hard just to bring the transaction to neutral, and you'll have to work harder yet to bring it to positive.

3. *Show the customer what you do have.* The customer has come to you because he or she wants you to solve a problem or take care

of a need. In most cases, as long as you are able to help, the person will buy.

Creative marketing: Taking the "Let me show you what we have" approach also develops a rapport with the customer, promotes customer service, and buys you time in finding out what problem needs to be solved.

4. *Show the customer or client that you care.* When you say no to a client, communication begins a natural death. Instead, start a conversation with your customer. This shows that you care.

For example, an appliance store owner consistently tried to match customer needs to his products. If someone wanted to buy a washer, he would ask the size of the family, the frequency of use, the amount washed daily or weekly, and similar questions. After he discovered the customer's lifestyle needs, he would show the person the machine that best fitted those needs. Sometimes the customer needed more washer than first thought; other times, he would suggest a less expensive model because that one best suited the person's lifestyle.

5. *Creative marketing.* Ask open-ended questions and let the customer talk. The individual will tell you a great deal about his or her lifestyle and needs. As we discussed in Chapter 3, the more demographics and "psychographics" you know about a customer, the better position you're in to sell your product or service. Rather than say no, use the customers' request as a challenge to provide something new for your customers. The opportunity opens up a new marketing base, invites potential new customers, and suggests a new avenue for income.

6. *Accept the challenge.* Not having a particular product on hand or not currently providing a service may be a blessing in disguise. It can be the basis of a new product or service. How many times have you developed a product or looked for a manufacturer or vendor to provide a new product, or done the research to offer a new service? Most small-business people have found themselves in this very position.

A local law firm, for example, puts on a business-conference extravaganza each year that brings in $3.5 million. The speakers are former presidents, chiefs-of-staff, and top entertainers. Ten years ago the conference started with 250 people; this year there were over 13,000 people in attendance. Just think about all the businesses that had to "challenge" themselves to provide the products and services needed for the conference. A no answer to a request from the organizers would have lost them the account.

Some of the challenges these small businesses encountered and met were:

- A tent large enough to hold the growing number of attendees. The vendor developed the largest tent in the world.
- Enough food to feed 13,000 attendees in thirty minutes. Subdivided main entree to one vendor, dessert to another, and beverages to a third vendor.
- Landscaping to include waterfalls, thousands of plants, and flowers. One nursery especially grows plants for this occasion.
- A large and complex sound system and television screens.
- Portable toilet to service men and women quickly at the highest level of hygiene.

Many of the companies that do business with this conference are challenged each year to make their products bigger and better. What if they had said "No, we don't do that"? They would have lost the opportunity for profits because they were afraid to be challenged.

Turn a Red Shirt Into a Blue Suit

Creative marketing is useful in all fields. Customers come in with an idea in mind, and you can use creative marketing techniques to turn a red shirt into a blue suit. Indeed, the more you let your customer talk, the more you will know how to solve the problem and consequently make a sale. Let's look at a few ways of turning a red shirt into a blue suit:

- *Consultant.* A builder from out of town calls and asks for a schematic map of a residential subdivision. After some discussion, you suggest photos of the area to include the neighborhood church, grammar school, high school, and other significant points that potential builders and homeowners would be interested in. In addition, you develop postcards for the client to send to potential customers.

- *Specialty advertising.* A business wants coffee mugs. After finding out the unit cost for the type of mug he wants, the owner ends up buying another specialty piece—wooden plaques—that turns out to be more expensive but serves his needs better.
- *Accountant.* A small accounting firm sends out business audiotapes monthly to its clients and to potential clients. The potential clients are now becoming customers because of the useful information on the tapes and the monthly "reminder" of the accountant.
- *Print shop.* A builder wants 100 decorated sheets. The print shop sells him 300 decorated sheets, since the style is being discontinued.
- *Appliance store.* A couple is ready to buy a white textured-front refrigerator until the salesperson shows them the better-looking shiny-front one with a $200 higher price tag.
- *Car dealership.* The last four vans an older couple have bought all were white. The salesperson took the couple's objection to buying another white van and asked what color striping and painting the customers would like. They now have a white van with blue and pink striping.

Pooling Your Small-Business Resources

Small businesses can join together for their mutual benefit. It's a great way to help one another and bring in more income all around. Two and a half years ago I developed the Small Business Marketing Program (SBMP). It is a way for no fewer than two local businesses and no more than five from different disciplines to get together every three weeks to share marketing strategies. I provide the sandwiches and a client provides the beverages. These small businesses do not have the finances individually to hire a marketing company. But by combining their efforts they are able to afford marketing. The Small Business Marketing Program includes:

- Participation in the program for a minimum of six months. This allows enough time to understand the business and start the marketing process.
- A newsletter combining all the businesses. Rather than costly individual mailing lists, the combined list increases contact with potential customers.
- A marketing trends report.
- Discounted seminars.
- Writing two press releases to the newspaper during each six-month period.
- Graphics for newsletters and flyers.
- Measured marketing results.

Another Example of Pooling Small-Business Resources

Local offices of vocational rehabilitation are operating under new federal regulations and the result has been limits on spending. To ensure continued income, a vocational rehabilitation agency developed a creative modular program whereby counselors work with several clients together on writing resumes, doing job research, and other areas of vocational rehabilitation rather than on a one-on-one basis, thereby keeping the costs under new regulatory limits. This is an example of a business creatively coming up with a program to ensure business for the company while helping cash flow restrictions imposed by legislation on the company. It's another example of creatively making the business work.

The Importance of Perceived Value

When developing your creative marketing schemes, it is paramount that you use the *perceived value* of an item or service to sell that product or service. Perceived value implies that the customer or client is getting more value for his or her money. Perceived value may be in the form of saving time or low financial expenditure for a product or service. Here are some examples of creative marketing with perceived value in mind:

• The health-care industry is in the midst of fierce competition, with HMOs, health-care facilities, health insurance companies, hospitals, and clinics all fighting for the consumer's dollar. The facilities that creatively market their health-care skills will be here decades to come.

One such facility is a family medical center in California, where a complete staff of doctors is available for any medical problem. How is this place different? In reality, it's not much different from the medical center across town, or the one two thousand miles away. However, this medical center is actively marketing by educating company executives and the movers and shakers in the city government about different health-care choices. The center brings in top-notch speakers in the industry for a complimentary breakfast at a local country club. The breakfast is by invitation only, which gets the attention of the invitees.

Perceived value: An opportunity to network with important people, the ego satisfaction of being invited to a prestigious country club, and the possibility of learning about health-care choices.

• A printing company offers a specific second color on print jobs each day of the work week, at no extra cost. This is a creative marketing concept because it implies extra value. The printer knows that if the customer likes the quality and service, and chances are very good that he or she will develop a "habit" of coming back. How often do you continue going to the same bank or video store because of a special ongoing offer?

Perceived value: Receive a two-color print job for the price of one. The second color will make your product look more professional and is likely to better capture the attention of your targeted audience.

• The Fish Grotto restaurant in San Francisco changes its menu fifty-two times a year. It will even fax the menu to you. It is also expanding its menu to include healthier choices.

Perceived value: The great variety of food and the low-fat health factor, and since some seafood is seasonal, the customer will not be disappointed by ordering something that is not available.

• A candy shop creatively markets its store by offering a coffee and cappuccino bar that also serves desserts. The aroma of baked foods and coffee, plus the decorated candies, invite customers to stay and try a few delectables.

Perceived value: A fun, calming, and enjoyable shopping experience.

- Bookstores today are fiercely competitive. Large discount chains make it difficult for independents to compete in price and selection. So small stores need to beat the discounters creatively and keep their customers coming back, even though those customers could get the same product across the street for less.

Earthlings, a wonderful bookstore in Santa Barbara, California, is always busy, with customers waiting to pay at the checkout lines. Because its atmosphere is friendlier, customers can review the large selection of books and tapes, munch on healthy food or drink cappuccino, read *The New York Times,* or just sit around the fireplace and read.

Perceived value: For just a little more per book, a place to read and be in a friendly environment.

- A gourmet shop that sells cookbooks, cooking utensils, and hard-to-find gadgets creatively brings in customers through its cooking kitchen. The managers invite chefs from around the county to come and teach customers everything from how to make white chocolate truffles to full-course meals. Even though the statistics show that more and more people are eating out, they also show that cookbooks are one of the fastest-growing areas of book sales. That probably means that people are going out to eat, but would enjoy cooking from scratch if they had the time. The culinary classes fit those double-edged needs: to learn to cook and to eat. The classes also showcase gadgets that are sold afterwards, and participants receive a 10 percent discount on all purchases the day of the cooking class.

Perceived value: For a brief time, a chance to satisfy one's need to cook or bake, to eat the showcased food, and to save time by being shown how to make the dish.

- A quaint tearoom in southern California serves breakfast and lunch during the week and special "romantic" dinners on Friday and Saturday nights, with classical music and dimmed lights. The shelves and tables show off antiques or reproductions that are gift items. People not only dine there but can also buy items to take home, including the table.

Perceived value: A way to shop and dine in a homey and

friendly atmosphere, or share a romantic meal with a loved one without taking the time to shop, cook, and clean up.

- A national woman's magazine creatively designed a fitness presentation featuring a fashion show with leading beauty, footwear, and athletic companies. It was called an evening of fitness, fashion, and fun.

Perceived value: A way to view fashions in sports clothing while saving time learning new beauty and fitness techniques.

- An international tennis shoe manufacturer targeted women for its footwear line by establishing a women's foot race on Mother's Day. The race was co-sponsored by a women's magazine.

Perceived value: A fun and healthy way to spend a special day.

- In Portland, Oregon, an accounting firm organized a statewide "adopt an emerging business" contest in conjunction with a law firm and a bank. The program was so popular it is now being tried in several other area cities. The accounting, finance, and legal experts received good public relations while demonstrating their skills and helping fledgling businesses.

Perceived value: An inexpensive way to get expert advice on growing a business.

- Ice cream maker Ben & Jerry's turned its search for a CEO into a marketing event. The company's "Yo! I want to be CEO" campaign asked for a 100-word essay and a lid from each candidate's favorite flavor of ice cream. The company received applications from all over the country and from at least a dozen other nations. In the process, they also sold a lot of ice cream.

Perceived value: A fun way to show how creative you are while looking for a job.

- A printing company in Ojai, California, developed a miniature game card to go with its services. Each time a customer uses a service with a minimum dollar amount, he or she gets the game card stamped. When finished, the card is put into a drawing, and the winner gets a trip to Japan to tour the printer's main headquarters.

Perceived value: Using the services of the print shop may lead to a free trip to Japan.

- An arts-and-crafts store in Los Angeles promotes savings for its customers during its Halloween Moonlight Madness Sale. Customers wearing a costume receive 30 percent off their purchase.

Perceived value: Shopping certain evening hours means saving 30 percent on arts-and-crafts items, all in the spirit of the holidays.

▪ Mattel, Inc., the creator of Barbie dolls, sold more than $500 million worth of dolls last year, and is now cashing in on the large trading-card business. Currently, the latter is a $400 million business, up from $25 million in 1980. Mattel says it is the first company to target trading cards to girls. "We already know that 15 to 20 percent of baseball-card sales are to little girls, and we know that little girls love Barbie," says Meryl Friedman, vice-president of marketing and product development for Mattel. But instead of batting averages, the cards tell key facts about Barbie: how she wore her hair and what outfit she wore to each party during her thirty-one year career.

Perceived value: A fun way to collect information about something or someone you like—plus there's always the chance that the cards will become collector's items.

▪ A small inn in northern California charged $24 a night but was not busy until the new owner raised the night's stay to $79, replaced the 1950s blond-oak furniture with "art" and "antiques," and began giving tours. "It was bloody magic," the owner says. "When the rooms were $24 we got complaints about how little they were. At $79 those same rooms became 'quaint,' 'charming,' and 'delightful.'"

Perceived value: Atmosphere and charm are worth paying more for.

▪ A few years ago, Tara was an abandoned house. Now it is the county's biggest tourist attraction and a country inn whose guests pay up to $318 a night to celebrate "the fondly remembered antebellum South." An entertainment entrepreneur's other attraction is The Old Order Amish Tour Farm, which boasts costumed guides and the "world's friendliest bunnies"—but not a real Amish person in sight.

Perceived value: Entertainment, reliving lost memories, and being in a charming place are worth paying for.

▪ Mr. Winner—the gentleman just described—also manufactures the Club, a device that locks a car steering wheel to prevent theft. The Club costs approximately $12 to make overseas, but sells here for $59.95. "We're not selling a piece of metal for $59.95; we're selling something that can protect a $20,000 investment." Winner's creative marketing includes an offer to pay owners up to $500 toward their insurance deductible if their cars are stolen within a year of buying the device.

Perceived value: A low-cost way to protect one's car.

• The owner of a video store in southern California and a film producer developed a unique way to get voters to register. An estimated 48 million households rent a video each month. What would be more convenient than to allow these people to register to vote when they pick up a video? They took the idea to the National Video Software Dealers' Association, and convinced them to participate in the drive. The stores benefit from the public relations in the process.

Perceived value: Being able to easily register to vote saves time.

• A local airport and a local car wash hooked up to offer air travelers the advertising message that said: "Your trip isn't over until your car is clean!" In conjunction with the airport, the first 1,000 cars to park five days or longer in the airport's long-term lot receive a free car wash.

Perceived value: A free car wash comes with the price of parking at the airport.

• A quick-print shop in Las Vegas, Nevada, grossed $5 million this year, or approximately nineteen times the industry average. "My paradigms are not the same as those that are consistent in this industry," the owner says. He markets his professional services as printing done on time and takes responsibility for proofreading jobs before they go to press. "Look, you don't go to a restaurant and have the waiter come out and say, 'The chef is ready to put your steak on. Do you want to come into the kitchen and see it's being done right?' Besides," he adds, "customers are terrible proofreaders."

Perceived value: Print work comes with bonus of free proofreading.

• The 17th St. Cafe, in Santa Monica, California, uses the back of its menu to tell a story about the restaurant as well as give "fascinating facts about our first five years":

We have fed over 600,000 people.
Jane has made over 4,000 desserts.

25,000 bottles of wine have been sold.

12,000 gallons of tortilla soup have been sold.

6,000 gallons of milk have been drunk.

We have 60 percent of our busboys still with us from opening day.

Perceived value: The story lends a charming touch and people feel that they will enjoy a home-cooked good meal.

Specialty Advertising That Has a Marketing Impact

Specialty advertising can have a tremendous impact, especially if the items are creative, are done with a sense of humor, and are functional as well. The following are creative uses of specialty items that made a dramatic difference for the companies that used them.

- *Stockbroker.* The stockbroker wrote a letter to her clients and included a self-dispensing lead pencil. Her clients called and asked for another.
- *Temporary Employment Service.* The clerical division handed out mirror compacts to guests at the agency's open house.
- *Safety and Claims Professional.* The man distributed a two-sided pen—yellow felt on one side and blue ink on the other, at a trade show. He also sent them to his clients and prospective clients along with a letter describing his services.
- *Marketing specialist.* During a five-minute presentation, I distribute a brochure and a fortune cookie. The fortune reads, "Ideas are only as good as their implementation"—which is also my company slogan.
- *Toy shop.* The owner mailed out invitations to people in the area. Inside the invitation was a balloon that, when blown up, showed the shop's name and "Bring in this balloon for a free toy."

Kenyon Sills, co-owner of a specialty advertising business, says "I try to be a problem solver—Tell me your problems, I'm here to fix them." Sills creates safety programs for businesses. A company was celebrating sixty years in business. The theme of the celebration was "Reflecting on the Past—60 years of safety and still shining." There was a shiny diamond placed on 2,000 T-shirts given to all the employees.

One of the safety programs Sills created was a "Safety Safari Handbook," with safety lessons presented in cartoon form. "You have to make safety more interesting and interactive," says Sills. "Safety can be boring, even though it's important. We developed a safety game in conjunction with the Olympic Games and called it 'Let the Safety Games Begin' and used the Olympic insignia with the company name in each of the five rings." Another safety program centered on sports: "Pitch for Safety" was printed on baseball caps.

When assessing specialty advertising items and programs, take advantage of seasons, holidays, and sports events. During January, February, and March, mugs that hold warm drinks are good; April, May, and June are excellent for hats, beach towels, and road atlases; July, August, and September are times for items that keep food cool; October, November, and December are when you bring out stadium blankets, thermoses for hot soup, jackets, and flashlights for daylight-savings changes.

Summary

Develop a creative mindset for your customers, clients, and employees. Do things in new ways to build customer satisfaction and increase cash flow.

You want to turn around *no* statements so they have positive results: talk to your clients about what they need, stay positive in your thoughts and speech, show customers what you do have, let customers or clients know that you care, and accept the challenge of providing a new service or product when the need arises.

You want to develop a business culture where creativity becomes an everyday activity of marketing. Customers and clients will then perceive your services and products as more valuable. Take advantage of the seasons, holidays, and sports events when creating specialty advertising items. The more creative and functional your items, the more you will be remembered.

8

Employees Are Your Number One Marketing Asset

Employees are a double-edged sword. They can be your number one marketing asset or your primary operating cost. Let's look at some numbers that put a reality check on the importance of hiring and keeping good employees.

According to *Recruiting Trends,* a human resources publication, managerial recruitment costs can equal 33 percent of a new recruit's first-year salary; training costs, 10 percent; and learning-curve costs, up to 50 percent[1]—that's 93 percent of the first year's salary. With these figures, it could potentially cost $56,000 to replace a typical $60,000-a-year regional sales manager. *Small Business Reports,* an industry newsletter, found that it may cost an employer more than $7,000 to replace a secretary.[2] Simply dismissing an employee can cost somewhere near $400—in hours spent terminating, paying benefits, creating recommendations, and listening to grievances.

The Bureau of National Affairs states that turnover rates for U.S. employees average around 12 percent.[3] However, this is a complex issue to calculate, as turnover may vary with location, department function, and time of year.

One way to figure your company or department's turnover rate is to add the number of employees terminated for all reasons during a specified time period and the number hired, and then divide this total by the work unit's average strength. A company that employs 500 people on average, and in one month lost one person owing to retirement and two by resignation, then hired two replacements, would have a turnover rate of 1 percent per month, or 12 percent per year:

$$(3 + 2)/500 = 1 \text{ percent} \times 12 \text{ months}$$

A cartoon by Cathy Guisewite says it all:

THE BOSS: "In the past month, the employees of this company have logged more personal long-distance phone calls than in any company in history. More unauthorized use of the fax . . . more pilfering of company supplies . . . more postage meter abuse . . . we've had the most coffee-room clean-up fights, more memo-defacing incidents, more parking-spot squabbles, more gossip and more gross practical jokes involving the copier. In short, we're number one."
EMPLOYEES: "Yeah, whistle, hoot, yeah, smack, yes!"
BOSS: "Not in any of the areas we're in business for, but we're number one."

Thus, turnover and recruitment are key factors in the Time-Marketing Equation. The question is how to transform a costly and time-consuming procedure into a business advantage. Remember, the *quality* of a company's marketing is measured by the responses customers get from employees with whom they come in contact. To succeed, any business must have the full support and cooperation of its employees. It must empower its employees to make decisions based on the company's mission statement. The mission statement cements business-customer relationships, and empowers employees to use it in strong creative self-expression. This is a time-positive marketing tool.

For example, State Farm Insurance has simplified its management considerably and created tremendous customer good-will in the process. Its slogan "Just Like a Good Neighbor . . ." empowers employees to make decisions, facilitating and streamlining customer contacts.

Employee Empowerment

You can read about the concept of empowerment in articles and books, and have probably heard about it in business seminars. I define *empowerment* as giving managers and employees the power to take care of their departments and customers in line with their responsibilities at the company. If an employee's responsibility is working with customers, then that individual needs to be allowed to sell the product or service and satisfy the customer any way possible, using creative ways to deal with customers.

For example, a customer-service specialist at Armstrong International, a manufacturing company, wrote a personal check for $150 to cover an invoice for a part because her customer needed that part immediately. When the customer paid, the employee was reimbursed.

My husband and I were having air-conditioning problems with our new minivan. The dealer's service department blamed it on a new type of air-conditioning fluid. Our salesman knew we were frustrated, and on his own ordered a loaner van for us until the problem was solved.

The manager of a department store took out his wallet to refund a customer when an electrical storm had caused a blackout and electrical cashboxes would not open.

Empowering your employees makes an impact on your profits, in the following ways:

- Employees buy into what they're doing. They feel they are making a difference, and take more initiative, creatively resolving many problems.
- When employees know that what they do affects the bottom line, they develop a pride in their company.
- Employees who feel responsible for their department and customers also feel more important. They see their work performance positively.
- Empowered employees build strong relationships with customers. The customers know that if anything goes wrong, their "empowered employee" can solve the problem.
- When employees are happier at their jobs, they tend to stay there longer.

Employee Participation

It's good marketing sense to involve your employees in all aspects of the business. One of the best ways for employees to understand what each department in a company does is to cluster employees from different departments and different jobs in order to achieve a mutual goal. This mutual goal may be to develop a new product or sales strategy. It may be to think of new ways to deal with customer-satisfaction levels and customer service. Or the employee cluster may just be a way to get people together to brainstorm ways to reduce operating costs.

Janey Cajer, a software programmer, gets together every other week with four other employees of the computer company where she works to brainstorm customer-satisfaction matters. She and her cluster group have been doing this for eight months and have come up with two new customer-satisfaction ideas that have been implemented: a demonstration software package rather than just a descriptive brochure and two 20-minute demonstration classes for each type of software. It is too early to see bottom-line results, but the group feels confident that the figures will reflect their efforts.

In a similar vein, Herman Miller Inc., a $793 million office-furniture manufacturer, has been involved with employee participation since 1950. The company's suggestion system leads to $12 million each year in cost savings.

Likewise, a law firm decided that it was receiving the same complaints from its clients over and over, even though business was healthy. The firm founded the Brainstorm Trust, whereby all employees and the three partners meet each month to brainstorm ways to eliminate, or at least lessen, the number of complaints.

During brainstorming sessions, have employees decide how they each can best market the company. Then have them develop a time line for doing so. For example, I am working with a company where each employee develops an eight-week marketing time line—The tasks each employee specifically will do in an eight-week period. A typical employee time line looks like this:

Name_____

The time-line needs to address the following topics:

Date   Description of Marketing

TIME LINE

October 12_____December 12
Jerry Jantzen, a telecommunications representative, developed his
time line as follows:

Jerry W.

October 12_____December 12

October	14 — Target new business start-ups for September and October
	15 — Visit city hall license department
	17 — Set up lunch with three telephone powerhouses
	26 — Set up appointments in one new territory
	31 — Lunch with "3"

November	4 — Follow-up letter with new business start-ups
	12 — Set one morning a week to be in office
	25 — Start the Solid project
	1 — Analyze new business start-ups
	7 — Analyze new territory

Employee Communication

Peter Drucker, management consultant and business guru, says
that the lack of effective communication within an organization is
a major reason for high turnover. This is especially true of communication between supervisors and their staff members, he claims.[4]

A study by Wick & Co., a human resources consulting company based in Wilmington, Delaware, surveyed 110 men and
women in Fortune 500 companies. They found that less than 10
percent cited money as a reason for possibly leaving their jobs.
More common factors in resignations are a poor relationship with
the boss, a negative work environment, lack of recognition, and
few opportunities for personal development and advancement.[5]

Sandra Kurtzig, chief executive officer for ASK Computer Systems, says, "People need to feel free to communicate what's on their minds. We constantly have meetings to get people communicating. At 'Lunch with Sandy,' which we hold periodically, employees can ask any questions they want."

Specifying the dates that certain functions need to be done accomplishes four important points: 1) It breaks down an otherwise large project into small, workable pieces, 2) It prevents procrastination, 3) It encourages pre-planning and focus, and 4) The time line ensures accountability.

Employee Attitudes and Morale

Companies are using storytelling as a way to instill in employees the correct business image and policies. David Armstrong, at Armstrong International, is a king of storytellers. In the last twenty-four months, Armstrong has penned almost eighty stories calling notice to particular employees as "champions of urgency, innovation and leadership." These accounts of excellence decorate the company's halls and walls, and each ends with a short comment on why the deeds are valued.

The surest way to know the culture of a company is to listen to the stories about its employees. Most people learn by example, and stories are examples. They teach acceptable behavior and encourage exceptional behavior.

To incorporate stories and real-life accounts of employee accomplishments, look within the company for the smallest deeds. Every employee, large or small, has a story to tell.

Key Points in Honoring Employees

- *Be sincere.* If you don't believe in commendations, don't do them. The accounts have to be true and sincere. You have to really believe that the employee has made a difference.
- *Be clear.* Think of what you want to get across—the essence of the story, the message.
- *Be specific.* Using facts and details lends credence, a real feeling of acknowledgement for the person involved.

- *Conclude with a moral.* State the lesson to be learned. Don't take it for granted. Depending on who reports the story, the account may have several lessons to be communicated.

The Well-Paid Employee

Barry Steinberg, of East Coast Direct Tire, knows that he needs to retain the best mechanics and alignment specialists if he is to keep his service promise (see Chapter 4). He goes to a headhunter to find his people. As a general rule, Steinberg pays his twenty-seven employees 15 to 25 percent above the industry standard. Labor costs amount to 28 percent of sales, so his commitment to having well-qualified technicians costs him more than $172,000 a year. But Steinberg sees this expenditure as an investment—fewer mistakes are made, and doing the job right the first time saves time and money. In addition, good employees are more self-reliant, so fewer supervisors are needed, which again translates to savings.

Flexibility Equals Productivity

Today's workforce is more diverse than ever before. Employees have more personal demands on their time, especially commitments to family. The business that acknowledges this situation and does something to ease the stress will also lower absenteeism and employee turnover, and increase productivity and loyalty to the company.

A study by the Child Care Action Campaign (CCAC), a New York City–based coalition of leaders in the child-care field, found that of 5,000 workers with young children at five Midwestern corporations, 48 percent of the women and 25 percent of the men felt that worries about child care made their work less productive. If other anxieties and stresses are brought into play—an aging parent, a sick child or spouse, a son or daughter moving back home—it would be safe to say that those percentages would increase dramatically. The CCAC estimates that businesses lose nearly $3 billion each year because of child-care–related absences.[6]

"Small companies might not have the hard dollars for [day

care] programs, but they can help out in ways that don't cost money," says Sue Bonoff-Seitel, president of Work and Family Connection, a consulting firm in Minnetonka, Minnesota.

Benefits consultants with Towers Perrin, New York, queried workers in focus groups and found that many employees would most like to see tuition assistance for their children as a new benefit. "We're hearing more and more that employees want this and need this," says Margaret Regan, a principal with Towers Perrin. "It's definitely a cutting-edge benefit for the 1990s."

Here are some ways that small businesses can motivate their employees and prevent high costs from closing their doors:

- *You still have a job.* Allow parental leave after a child has been born or adopted; let employees take time off to be with a sick, aging parent or a hospitalized spouse. A small business may not be able to afford paid parental leave, but knowing the job is waiting upon return keeps employees happy at only the cost of temporary help.

- *You don't have to say why.* Because of other commitments, whatever they may be, employees may need a certain number of personal days off each year. They do not have to give a reason why. Offer these to keep employees on your staff.

- *Choose your times.* Flexible time schedules are one of the best marketing tools available. Employees are passionate about a company that cares about them as people. One of the best ways to show this concern is through flexible work schedules. See if it is possible to rotate employees so that some arrive thirty minutes to an hour early and leave thirty minutes to an hour later once or twice a week. Could two people do the same job and split the salary and benefits? A little bit of creativity goes a long way in making employees happy at no extra cost.

Summary

Employees can be your number one marketing asset, particularly if you empower them to make decisions that keep or attract customers and clients. Empowered employees buy into what they're doing, have pride in the company, feel important, have perceived customer influence, and display lower turnover.

Employee morale is raised when owners or managers recognize the valuable contributions of employees. One way to do this is by publicizing stories and accounts of exceptional work. The five key attributes of effective stories are that they (1) are sincere, (2) are clear, (3) are specific, (4) focus on small deeds or actions, and (5) have a moral or lesson.

Other ways to increase employee motivation and productivity, thereby increasing cash flow, are by effective employee communications, and flexible time schedules.

Notes

1. Kent R. Davies, "The Exchange Rate," *Executive Female.* November/December 1990, p. 28.
2. Ibid.
3. Ibid.
4. Ibid., p. 29.
5. Ibid., p. 29.
6. Jane Easter Bahis, *Entrepreneurial Woman*, April 1991, p. 56.

9

The Power of Good Relationships

The single most important thing your customers or clients can give you is repeat business. The single most important thing you can give your customers or clients is the feeling that you care. Relationships are everything in business. They lay the groundwork for future sales, for profits, for new directions that the business may take.

The second half of the 1990s and beyond mark an era of marketing based on genuine customer involvement, good communication of information, and creation of new markets. This "new" type of marketing is referred to as *Relationship marketing.* As Regis McKenna describes in his book, *Relationship Marketing,* "Successful companies must be willing to adapt their products and services to fit customers' needs. Forging a new relationship between customer and company, the effective marketer will serve as integrator, bringing the customer into the company as an active participant in the development of these goods and services."[1]

The old style of marketing called for manipulating the customer and saw the marketplace as a limited entity, divided into market shares or slices of the pie. This approach was *marketing* driven. It used a bag of marketing tricks and promotions in order to sell products and services.

The new marketing paradigm is customer driven, or *market* driven. This approach suggests that you promote your company, your products, and your services to become the leader in your field. And you use your relationships with customers, vendors, suppliers, and even competitors to make that happen. When you lead in marketing, you've won. Leadership is ownership, and leaders are people who know the importance of building relationships.

This new market-driven approach calls for good communications—between your business and your customers and between your company and the marketplace. Your products and services are created from and modified by the results of your communications—your relationships with your customers and the marketplace.

The marketplace is not static. Every day there are changes brought about by new technology, a changing labor market, and other transitional forces. Strong business relationships are the foundation for making adjustments and innovations. Standard promotions, customary advertising, and the old manipulative approach to marketing will not keep your clients coming during the storm.

Techniques for a Market-Driven Approach

- Ask your customers frequently how you might make changes to products or services that would make them more user-friendly.
- Brainstorm with customers, vendors, and others on how to streamline the company.
- See your customers and employees as your business partners.
- Keep a dialogue with everyone you do business with—employees, suppliers, manufacturers.
- Communicate news of changes and developments, using newsletters, bulletins, letters, and brochures.

Your Business Relationships

In its report "Know the Buyer Better,"[2] Penton Publishers in Cleveland, Ohio, noted the following findings as reviewed in the April 1991 issue of *Business Marketing*.

- Seventy-two percent of respondents said their companies operate by having people do more with less; 28 percent are doing more with the same number of staff.
- Fifty-five percent report more interaction between compa-

nies and their vendors—32 percent report the same level of contact; and 12 percent report less contact.

- There has been an increase in women decisionmakers at companies—in 1990, 64 percent of buyers were men and 36 percent were women, compared to 72 percent men and 28 percent women in 1983.
- Fifty-one percent of businesses say they want to establish a partnership relationship with their vendors; 34 percent want technical advice and current information, and 28 percent want more honesty and integrity.

Whether as a small-business owner you are a supplier or a customer, you need to understand the way people establish partnerships, how they solicit and dispense technological information, how they convey honesty and integrity.

There are three ways people communicate and learn: visual, auditory, and kinesthetic. Let's look at each of these.

- *Visual.* Most Americans are visual learners. They learn from books, videos, and eye contact with others. Our world is largely visual. You frequently hear people say "See you later," "Looks good to me," "View this," "I see what you mean." Key communication words such as *see, look, clear, picture, notice,* and *appear* are references to the visual.
- *Auditory.* It is estimated that fewer than 7 percent of Americans are primarily auditory. These people are not comfortable with eye contact. They learn best by listening, and they like to sit in the back of the room. Their choice of words may go something like this: "Let's discuss it," "Listen up," "Talk to you later," "Sounds good to me," "I hear you started tennis." Key communication words such as *hear, listen, say, tell, sound,* and *discuss* are references to the auditory.
- *Kinesthetic.* These people are feeling communicators and learners. They tend to be huggers and touchers. They will say "This gives me something to grasp on," or "What does it feel like?" Key communication words such as *feel, handle, grasp, touch, excite,* and *share* are references to the kinesthetic.

A large part of any business is communicating your appreciation to your customers. Often a simple thank-you binds a customer, a vendor, or a prospect's receptionist and helps you get what you need. Saying thank-you before, during, and after a sale becomes a powerful, no-time-wasted marketing tool. Properly executed, it almost guarantees that your contact will deal with you again and again.

This can be as simple as a telephone call. It also means sending the thank-you gifts that are distinctive enough to survive the waste basket. One example is a solid brass yo-yo with the inscription, "This is the only yo-yo you'll get from us." Susan Jenkins, a management-placement consultant, regularly searches for items with which to say thank-you.

Forward-thinking businesses not only thank customers but also their suppliers. This nicety makes the wheels turn easier and also helps develop, nurture, and sustain good relationships. Thank-you is part of good communication, and good communication is a never-ending business and is a good way to stay in contact with your customer or client.

Let's look at some ways to effectively stay in contact in visual, auditory, and kinesthetic ways.

- *Send a button.* The U.S. Postal Service mailed a postcard with an aluminum pin that reads "I'm Indispensable—The U.S. Postal Service Salutes Secretaries Week." Similarly, I send "Where Did the Time Go?" buttons because that is the title of my first book. The receivers love to wear the button.

TIME TIP: *Choose a low cost product from your inventory or develop "Ten Tips to Successful Marketing" or "Ten Tips to Successful . . ." (within your discipline), and make copies of this with your business logo on heavier bond, and send or hand-deliver these items as appropriate. The client finds these as added value, plus, it shows that you care and gives you another reason to keep in touch.*

- Visual communicators will love the buttons.
- Auditory communicators will enjoy the buttons more if they make a sound or say something.
- Kinesthetic communicators will enjoy the buttons most if

you hand-deliver them or send a personal note along with them.

- *Order enough.* Overprint the number of newsletters you need. Jason, a small-business owner, is starting a subscription newsletter. He printed an additional 2,000 copies so he can send them as thank-you's and to interest new subscribers. The additional cost is $150, while the time it takes to print 2,000 more newsletters is the same.
  - Visual communicators will like clean graphics.
  - Auditory communicators will prefer the newsletter on tape.
  - Kinesthetic communicators will like the feel of textured paper.

TIME TIP: *Choose one or two specialty advertising pieces and send or hand-deliver these items as appropriate. It is less costly and less time-consuming to make one large order. Two years ago I ordered fortune cookies with the message "Ideas are only as good as their implementation—The Marketing Source." I have had them for over two years and they are still relatively fresh.*

- *Send Thanksgiving cards.* After all, you are thanking your customers, vendors, and staff for doing business with you. Christmas cards easily get lost in the shuffle, but Thanksgiving cards stand out.

  - Visual communicators will enjoy the colorful cards.
  - Auditory communicators will prefer a telephone call.
  - Kinesthetic communicators will like the warm feelings communicated.

TIME TIP: *Keep an updated list of all your business contacts. Hire a temp to hand-address the envelopes. You can sign the cards during slow periods of the day or when you are waiting on the phone.*

- *Make random database calls.* Look through your database and randomly call people you haven't spoken to for a while. Call just to say "Hi."

- Visual communicators remember what you look like.
- Auditory communicators remember previous conversations.
- Kinesthetic communicators prefer an in-person visit or to receive something they can touch or grasp.

TIME TIP: *Set aside thirty minutes three times a week to do this. You will be surprised at the number of people who end up doing business with you again and the deals you set in motion.*

Relationships Are for the Long Haul

Most business people are in for the long haul. And this situation is excellent for establishing business relationships. For the 1990s and beyond, "company attitudes and plans will move from a short-term to a long-term focus," says William Carey Jr., founder of Corporate Resource Development, Inc.

Roger Cavater, a stockbroker for over twenty-five years, does exceptionally well. On the other hand, Mike Jackson has been a partner in an accounting firm for over thirty years and is not doing well. What makes for the difference? The answer is not in years of experience but in staying in contact with clients over time. Roger kept in contact constantly with his clients while he pursued new business. Mike's firm was so busy and well established that it worked well with the clients it had but did not market to new clients.

Pass Out Those Cards

Customers often don't know the scope of what you do or produce. Indeed, the people closest to you frequently do not really know the depth of services you provide or all the products you offer. Your immediate clients and customers know what you do for them, but in many cases they do not know what other things you can do.

For example, an advertising agency in North Carolina develops ads and also puts together public relations campaigns. One of the photographers the agency does business with on brochures and newsletters asked if he also did P.R. "I couldn't believe Don asked me that," commented Jerry Shones, the vice-president. "A third of our business is in public relations. It hit me hard that I must not be communicating very well what I do. He also asked me to send him a few business cards so that he could pass them on. It also occurred to me that a good marketing idea would be to send all my clients and customers a few extra business cards."

You may want to send a few extra business cards in with your billing once or twice a year, or include a few business cards in a thank-you-for-your-business note.

I recently attended a meeting with an attorney, an accountant, and four board members of a charity organization. The attorney and accountant were developing the documents for nonprofit status for the organization. However, the first thing they both did once they sat down at the table was to pass out their business cards. I thought it was quite interesting the subtle way they handled it and how professional they were for doing so. The marketing push here is, if you know who I am and like me, and have my business card handy, you might refer business to me.

Vendors as Partners

You have developed relationships with a variety of vendors in the process of doing business. The more successful you are, chances are the more successful they are too. It becomes clear, then, that it is to your advantage to ask them for advice, and to brainstorm with them on new ways of doing things. Businesses in the future will be asking more of vendors. States William Carey of Corporate Resource Development, "Vendors will no longer see selling as one transaction after another. Instead, there will be a shift to advisory relationships. We'll see more partnerships and joint ventures in a more difficult economic environment. The results will be complementary relationships between companies with different areas of expertise."

Ciba Corning Diagnostics Corporation, based in Medfield, Massachusetts, is an industrial designer. The company designs by interviewing purchasers, end-users, maintenance workers, and anyone else who might work with its equipment. The designers not only get invaluable information this way but develop a loyal following as well.

Richard Golden, president and CEO of D.O.C. Optic Corporation, based in Southfield, Michigan, says "A lot of upfront market research dramatically improves your business's chances of success." Golden tracks industry trade publications and trends in his industry by "talking with our suppliers, store managers, and customers [to help] confirm the trends." These kinds of sharing relationships can make the difference between profit and loss.

Build a Strong Relationship With a Few Vendors

There was a time when businesses would keep hundreds of vendors on their supplier list. Because of competition and the race to streamline operations, the fewer the vendors now the better. It is less costly and allows a business to develop a stronger relationship with a few important vendors. In return, these vendors are more likely to negotiate better deals and services. After all, the loss of your business would mean a substantial loss for them as well.

David Auld of Baxter Healthcare Corporation, says, "We used to have thirty to forty vendors for corrugated cardboard; now we have three. We have a plant in North Carolina that puts out more than 1 million units [of intravenous solution] a day, but the plant doesn't have more than an hour or two of corrugated on hand because of the just-in-time delivery arrangements that we have with our vendors."

Customers as Partners

Here are a few ideas on working with your customers to develop a partnership that is advantageous for both sides.

- As discussed in Chapter 10, any type of community service tie-in is positive for both parties.
- A retail dress shop in Lake Tahoe, Nevada, once a year, asked its customers to bring in old clothes and receive a 10 percent discount on new purchases. The store then contributed the old clothes to a local charity.
- Federal Express, which normally ships packages, is now of-

fering to also handle clients' logistics processes, from warehousing and inventory management to order processing and
customer billing.

- Goodyear Tire & Rubber Company stores sell not only their
own tires but also those of their competitors, mount them on
wheels and supply them to customers.

Baxter Healthcare Corporation sells medical supplies to hospitals. Now, with its new partnering concept, it helps its customer
hospitals use the supplies more effectively. In addition, Baxter
works with its vendors more closely. "We used to take the attitude
that we would deal with vendors at arm's length and just send
them the specification," says David Auld, senior vice-president of
quality leadership. "We didn't even want them in the plant because we were afraid that they would disclose our operations to
our competitors. We are now totally open, and we even ask some
of our qualified vendors to come in and participate in the R & D
process and lend us their expertise."

Likewise, Kenyon Sills, co-owner of an advertising specialty
agency, says, "We handle more and more services for our customers, like distribution and tracking. We try to be problem solvers.
'Tell me your problems—we're here to fix them.'"

Build a Strong Relationship With a Few Clients

The key factor in marketing for the 1990s and beyond is focusing
on a smaller sector of customers, but selling them more services or
products. Chances are good that 20 percent of your customers
bring in 80 percent of your profit. If you focus on sales only, you
may be working very hard, but spinning your wheels and not making much money. Remember, keep profits as your guiding light.

A quick-print business owner goes out *in person* to his 150
largest customers, thanks them for their business, and asks them
two questions: How can we improve things, and What kind of
printing are you buying elsewhere that you're not getting from us?
The owner found that continuous forms was the answer he heard
a lot. "So we bought a short-run continuous-form press" and today
the company sells continuous forms to 60 percent of its existing
commercial accounts.

Understand Your Client's Business

For businesses whose customers are also in business—in other words, if you are a vendor—then the more you understand your client's business, the more easily you can match your services and products to your client's needs. Says Jim Dull, Ernst & Young's director of consumer-products consulting for the Great Lakes region, "In the last couple of years, increasing numbers of companies have replaced the salesperson's visit and now take a team approach to contacting their most important customers."

So your partnership relationships with your customers may be more than a one-on-one situation. Rather, you may encounter a team approach covering different angles of the business. This team approach may well make a big difference in sales. "The team might include someone from traffic planning, from warehousing, from information systems, and from customer service . . . making it a much broader effort than before," says Dull.

Summary

Building solid relationships with customers, vendors, and competitors is a vital part of doing business today. The new market-driven business approach looks at owning the market through informed leadership and relationship building.

Remember that, when building relationships, you need to take advantage of visual, auditory, and kinesthetic communications, since people relate in these three different ways. Use buttons, newsletters, random database calls, cards, and food to reinforce relationships.

Since you are in for the long haul, become knowledgeable about your customers' businesses and make both your customers and your vendors your partners.

Notes

1. Regis McKenna, *Relationship Marketing* (Reading, Mass.: Addison-Wesley, 1985).
2. Penton Publishers (Cleveland), *Know the Buyer* report as reviewed in *Business Marketing,* April 1991.

10

Small Business and the Community

Almost nothing puts a business name before the public (and creates good-will) like community service. Companies act as toy-collection headquarters for underprivileged kids, sponsor sports teams, participate in local fairs, help with community tree planting, raise funds for historical societies, and spearhead recycling campaigns. A good example of community service was the Candice Bergen-Sprint tree-planting campaign. It doesn't make any difference that Sprint was planting trees to get your business. What is important is that, out of thousands of businesses, this one was doing something good.

Thinking Community Service

A visionary association, Business for Social Responsibility (BSR), is gaining national support. Member companies include Levi Strauss, Stride-Rite, Ben & Jerry's, and Reebok. The businesses involved in BSR want to increase environmental accountability, create a friendly employee workplace, and directly help their communities, locally, regionally, and nationally.

Most community service projects require little management time yet generate tremendous community good-will and numerous publicity opportunities. Many years ago I owned a women's fashion boutique. We developed several community tie-ins with the store and received community attention as a by-product. For example, we created a travel-fashion brunch auction with a local travel agency. The proceeds from the auction went to a community charity and everyone benefited—community, employees, clients, and the business.

Another time we had a Queen of Hearts fund-raiser to benefit the American Heart Association. I thought that the idea would be fun and a play on words. The event drew new customers, and again it was a win-win situation.

Years ago we had customers bring in old clothing in exchange for 10 percent off the price of a new garment. We built a lovely relationship with the local American Cancer Society thrift shop, which resulted in my serving on their board of directors for two years.

We also put together a fashion-show auction for the Arthritis Association to raise funds for their proposed Aquatic Pool Center. It was an excellent fund-raiser and such fun that it became a yearly event. We auctioned off clothing on the runway. Years later they built the center and etched my name as a contributing member on a plaque at the entrance.

Make the time. "Thinking" time is required to develop community service events. As you read the newspaper, watch television, or speak to people, notice what can be done to make your community a better, safer, or economically healthier place to live. Becoming active in community events brings you positive visibility, leaves you with a good internal feeling, and gets you new customers. You can make a difference!

Anita Roddick, founder of The Body Shop, an international manufacturer and retailer of quality skin, hair, and color cosmetic products, is committed to using her now more than 1,200 shops as vehicles for social change. Every employee of The Body Shop is encouraged to spend up to four paid hours a month on a community service project. These projects are as varied as local communities across America—ranging from building a Habitat for Humanity house to bringing meals to AIDS patients to river clean-ups and tutoring. Another example of community care is The Body Shop "community store" located in Harlem. As an effort to help revitalize the area, The Body Shop will donate 50 percent of pre-tax profits or 5 percent of sales (whichever is greater) to the community. The remaining 50 percent of profits or another 5 percent of sales will be placed in a fund to open another community store.

Dayton Hudson gives back 5 percent of its taxable profits to the communities where it does business. It is estimated that since 1946, when the company started this community program, more than $200 million has been contributed. The company's brochure says, "We make contributions in two areas where we believe we can make a real difference: social service programs and local arts. Our grants encourage young people and adults to complete their education, be self-reliant, and find and keep good jobs."

Tying Marketing to Community Service

During the Persian Gulf War, there was mention in a local newspaper about Gottschalks' offering relief for soldiers. Gottschalks is a multichain, family-owned business in northern California. As described in an ad in the paper, the store offered financial relief from bills to the families of soldiers and reservists called to duty in the Mideast crisis. As mentioned in a column in the paper, "By this act of social responsibility, Gottschalks earned appreciation and support and I will demonstrate this with my wallet. They have earned my respect and my business." What was the added cost to the store? The cost of the advertisement. However, that becomes a financial plus that returns in the form of future customers.

As another example, Long's Drug Store, a multichain California drugstore, opened its doors for free merchandise to a family whose husband and father, a deputy sheriff, had been killed in a neighborhood incident. This act of kindness received tremendous positive publicity.

As a community service, I started a Self-Esteem Council to promote self-esteem in children and young adults. A percentage of the profits from my first book, *Where Did The Time Go? The Working Woman's Guide to Creative Time Management,* established the seed money. We created a yearly fund-raiser, "Tux and Tales," and hope to provide this event in several cities, with the money raised in each area given to community self-esteem programs.

We were able to get contributions of food, beverages, legal and CPA services, and volunteer help for entertainment, setup, and cleanup. The largest portion of time involved setting up the non-profit organization and establishing the first fund-raising event. The actual costs of the project were dwarfed in comparison to the publicity the involved businesses received. The evening was a success for everyone in attendance.

A recent political fund-raiser designed a family fundraising event. A family entertainment park donated the evening specifically for the event, and the admission ticket read, "Bring the whole family." The family ticket admitted all immediate members of a family—mom and dad, kids, grandma and grandpa. Included in the ticket were dinner, drinks, unlimited free rides and games, plus 50 free tokens, good for prizes. The family ticket was $100. However, the value of the ticket exceeded its cost, as did the single ticket. The cost of the benefit was the cost of providing food and beverages.

Of course, make sure you send news releases to all local newspapers before and after any community event. The value of this kind of marketing—to you—occurs only when the community knows what good you are doing.

Here are more ideas for community service that take little to no time:

- Businesses that offer tours of factories or manufacturing plants can have each guest bring a used newspaper or magazine in exchange for a "pass" to the facility. This promotes recycling.
- A health-care facility gives preventive health tips as part of its advertising. The messages are simple, easy, and give the facility a caring image. For instance, one message stressed the value of walking at least three times a week. The message advised people as to the aerobic way to walk, the pulse rate to be achieved, and safety tips to avoid injury. Other tips have stressed proper diet, stress reduction methods, and tips for lowering blood pressure.
- The real estate association in a mid-size city collects canned goods for the needy during the holiday season. To obtain maximum exposure and keep it fun, they stack the cans in a

triangle in the middle of the office. To publicize this event, the organization calls the local newspaper for a photographer or sends its own photos to the paper.

- A small advertising agency chooses a nonprofit organization each year to lend its services in creating an advertising strategy or collateral material—for example, brochures and flyers. They do not charge for their time or for creative production, only for actual costs.
- Local builders, interior designers, and architects created playhouses called Creating Dreams for Children, which were auctioned to raise funds to build a house as part of the national organization, Habitat for Humanity.

There's no end to ideas for community service projects. For example, develop a food drive in February for Valentine's Day, with the slogan, "We love you, Valentine" or "From our hearts to yours." Likewise, fruits and vegetables are abundant during the summer. Develop a fresh fruit and vegetable food drive for food shelters.

Take a percentage of your net profits for a certain period of time and give them to your favorite group or family.

Sherry Poe, at Rÿka, a tennis-shoe manufacturer, started the ROSE (Regaining One's Self-Esteem) Foundation, dedicated to ending violence against women (800-255-2952, ext. 125). The company puts tags describing the foundation inside its shoe boxes. Looking at two brands of tennis shoes, all things being equal, which pair do you think most women would chose? Not only do these shoes make your feet feel good but they also make you feel more "comfy" knowing that you have contributed to a worthwhile cause.

A local newspaper prints a circular around the holidays, called the Book of Dreams, which lists families that need special items such as a wheelchair for an elderly person or bicycle for a teen to get to work. A single mother with two children to support needed clothes to look for work, plus day care for her children. The community pitched in and provided her with several dozen second-hand outfits. In addition, a church invited her to enter her children into its day-care center at no charge for an entire year. Almost everyone who is profiled in the report receives what is needed.

An amusement park developed an Academic Excellence Program for grades 1 through 8. Children bring in their report cards within six weeks of issue and receive free tokens for A's and B's. This same amusement park also designs "fun-raisers" for schools, churches, civic organizations, and teams. The park gives the organizations a $5 rebate on each $12.99 wristband it sells.

Your business is an extension of who you are—your likes, your dislikes, your passions. Develop a new charity event around your business quarterly or twice a year, and make the successful ones yearly events. These events will not only bring attention to your business in the form of free publicity but will increase community and employee good-will and will, in the long run, increase profits. Of course, there is no price tag on giving something back to the community that supports your services or products and that gives you such good feelings and peace of mind.

Getting the Message Across

The Business Enterprise Trust was founded in 1989 by eighteen prominent leaders in American business, academia, labor and the media. The Trust "seeks to shine a spotlight on acts of courage, integrity and social vision in business—acts that advance the compelling principle that businesses which serve their constituencies in creative and morally thoughtful ways, in the long run, also serve their shareholders best." Each year since 1991, the Trust has honored business people who combine sound management with social consciousness with its Business Enterprise Awards. The nonprofit organization receives some of its income selling educational and training packages featuring videos, monographs, and case studies of each year's winners. For nomination forms or further information, contact the Trust at 204 Junipero Serra Boulevard, Stanford, California 94305; (415) 321-5100, fax (415) 321-5774.

Here are some of the criteria for the awards, taken from their brochure.

- Employees whose courage and determination result in new, more enlightened business practices;
- Entrepreneurs who demonstrate social vision by creating new products, services or forms of corporate organization that address important social needs;
- Managers who show moral thoughtfulness, commitment to principle, and sensitivity to the needs of business's many stakeholders in making difficult decisions;
- Business leaders who resist pressures for short-term performance in serving the genuine long-term interests of both shareholders and society;
- Business persons who uphold important business principles and serve the common good, particularly in the face of substantial personal or corporate risk;
- Any business person who struggles productively with the natural tension between corporate profitability and social needs.

A recent award recipient was Finast stores. According to its citation, "Defying conventional wisdom, Finast built or renovated eleven supermarkets in the inner-city of Cleveland, demonstrating that business can operate profitably in a distressed urban neighborhood. Through resourceful management and active community outreach, Finast has improved its operating efficiency, profitability and market share while spurring economic development."

As president and CEO of Springfield ReManufacturing Corporation, Jack Stack, another award winner, initiated a highly original management system that required all employees to learn and use monthly financial statements to improve job performance. "By encouraging workers to contribute their own creativity and intelligence, Stack rescued a failing manufacturing plant, launched eight new companies and spawned a growing national network of worker-empowered businesses."

A third winner, Gail Mayville, of Ben & Jerry's, demonstrated extraordinary initiative and imagination in pushing her company to create a more aggressive company-wide recycling program that benefited both the company and the environment. "Her commitment, creative insights, dogged research and determined follow-through are models of the qualities needed to help business address social issues." Mayville has now become a national recycling expert.

Remember: Only work with people you want to help, not because it is the thing to do. Your passion and excitement for the project, and those of your employees, will come through in your work and increased profits will show up on the bottom line.

Summary

Tying your marketing strategies to community service puts your company before the public and creates good-will. Getting the message to the public requires letting the media and your customers know before and after each event or program, through news releases and flyers. Become involved in the issues and services you and your staff feel are important. Your passion and excitement for these activities will encourage their success in the community and in your business.

11

Trade Show Marketing— Strutting Your Stuff

"Trade show participation is the linchpin to a truly integrated marketing strategy," says Steve Sind, President and CEO of the Center for Exhibition Industry Research (formerly the Trade Show Bureau). Senior management has recognized the value of exhibit marketing. In a survey of thirty-six marketing directors representing twelve industries, 73 percent of respondents reported that their presidents or CEOs participated in trade shows. These senior executives take part in the following activities: 89 percent discuss business with industry allies; 88 percent evaluate the competition; 85 percent participate in sales meetings with key accounts; 71 percent conduct informal market research with customers; and 65 percent discuss business with competitors' executives.

Trade shows can save a small business an enormous amount of time by generating qualified leads. In fact, there are only two main reasons why businesses do not get the full marketing results of a trade show: (1) they do not qualify trade-show responses and (2) there is no consistent follow-up. Trade show research states:

- A field representative usually reaches four to five prospective clients per day. Put that same salesperson on the exhibit floor, and he or she averages five qualified leads per hour, or thirty-five in a seven-hour day.
- A sales lead generated by any source other than a trade show requires an average of 4.3 calls to close. Generate that lead at a trade show, and 50 percent of the sales can be closed in just one field call.

- The cost of obtaining a qualified trade show contact is $142, compared to $259 for a field sales call.

Despite spending more than $25 billion on trade shows in 1991, small businesses do not understand this medium. You, as an exhibitor, need to create a workable plan that includes responsibility lists, timetables, and objectives so that you will get the most out of every show.

Remember: trade show attendees come first and foremost because they are looking for something new that they can use in their business, that offers an advantage over competition, or for any number of other reasons. The following Time-Marketing points will guide you to more successful exhibiting. These points have further been divided into three areas: pre-show marketing, marketing during the show, and post-show marketing.

Selecting the Right Trade Show

You want to select a trade show that will best serve your business interests and those of the customer. There are several good reference sources:

- The *Tradeshow Week Data Book,* published by *Tradeshow Week,* crosslists thousands of shows geographically, chronologically, alphabetically, and by industry classification.
- *Successful Meetings* publishes *Tradeshows & Exhibits Schedule,* which is a cross-listed directory.
- *Exhibitor* magazine publishes "Aisle View," a monthly newsletter of tips, tactics, and how-to's for the small and beginning exhibitor.
- The National Association of Exposition Managers in Aurora, Ohio,
- The International Exhibits Association in Springfield, Virginia,
- The Exhibit Designers and Producers Association in Milwaukee, Wisconsin.

Save time by checking the Trade Show Bureau's Exposition Validation Council (EVC) report, which provides detailed information about each show, including potential attendance and audience breakdown as well as attendees' job classifications and geographical distributions.

TIME TIP: Check the audience breakdown carefully. Make sure you work with the right market. That will save considerable time and money later. Investigate a minimum of sixteen weeks before exhibit and show date.

Target Market—Whom Do You Want to Come?

Do you want an international, national, or regional audience? Is your service or product suited for a specific theme, such as women-owned retail stores, or a general theme, as for all women in business? Once you have decided *whom* to target, then you can develop collateral material that is tailor-made to that group. If the target is women in business or home-based businesses, for example, then you need to research the specific area to give statistics and real benefits that will solve that group's problems. Once you have decided what these benefits are, then you can use them in your hand-out literature and in your invitations.

The 16 Percent Rule

Industry research and exhibit surveys have established that only 16 percent of a total show audience is interested in a single product line or service exhibited at that show.[1] If the projected audience is 3,000, multiply that by 16 percent to get the number of show participants (480) who potentially will be interested in your product or service. Also, take into consideration the "waste factor"—people in this group who are only curious about your product or service. There is usually a 20 percent waste factor. For example, in a show drawing 3,000, you need to plan on talking seriously to 384 show participants.

TIME TIP: Go over the 16 percent rule several times and decide cost-effectiveness and number of potential targeted leads. This will ensure that you apply time and energy in exactly the right way. Remember, do this a minimum of sixteen weeks before exhibit show date.

Set Measurable Goals

What do you want to accomplish at the show? There are several ways to look at this. First, your goal can be to gain a certain number of qualified sales leads; to sign up a dollar amount of sales; to get three media stories about your product or service; to test-market a new or revised product or service; to network and meet particular business owners in a specific trade; or to increase your database for direct mail. You need to make these goals *qualitatively* measurable, or you won't be able to measure your success.

TIME TIP: *Ask employees to brainstorm the types of setup that will help them reach their goals. Your schedule now is fourteen weeks.*

Develop a Budget

Trade shows, if planned for properly and followed up, are an excellent investment for small businesses. Some areas to remember to budget are booth space, setup and dismantling, specialty advertising give-aways, freight and transportation, audiovisual items, electrical and plumbing equipment, telephone service, collateral materials, personnel expenses, graphics, carpeting, advertising, airfare and hotel costs, and the exhibit space itself.

Once you have determined your costs, develop a worksheet for analyzing your dollar results: What is your return on investment (ROI)? ROI equals total sales volume divided by total show expenses. What is your cost per lead? This is equal to the total show expenses divided by the leads generated and so on. When it comes to media coverage, figure out the cost for an equal amount of advertising space. The total cost per exposure should equal total show expenses divided by total number of show participants.

TIME TIP: *Plan your specialty advertising and promotions six to twelve months in advance and include trade show marketing.*

This will give you more buying power with less money. These pro-
motional ideas will also serve as "holiday" gifts.

Trade Show Logistics

Carefully read through your trade show kit. Select a booth where
you think you will get the most traffic and feel that it will be a
good investment.

Select your booth features—electrical and phone service,
freight handler and shipper—and make hotel and travel plans.

TIME TIP: *Hanne Bentley, vice-president of Inline Inc., a*
wholesale housewares and upholstery distributor and importer in
Austin, Texas, always prepares a "meticulous list with contact
names and phone numbers of customs brokers, freight haulers,
show account reps, show labor orders—everything. That way, if
something doesn't turn up or your booth is not right, you know
exactly who's responsible." At this point your schedule is twelve
weeks before the show.

Send Out Invitations

To obtain results, you must send out invitations stating your booth
number and news of some new services or product you'll be sharing with your clients or prospects. The invitations need not be expensive. A colorful or interesting postcard takes less time and
money to produce and mail. If you want to contact hard-to-reach
people, stamp "Requested Information" on the envelope. This
should help get the invitation into the prospect's hands, rather
than into the waste basket.

According to the Trade Show Bureau, the number one reason
people decide to attend a trade show is because they've received
an invitation from an exhibiting company or sales representative.[2]
Share the information with potential clients who *want to know,*
rather than send a mass mailer to those you hope will want to
know about your new product or service. Allen Konapacki, president of Incomm International, suggests that spending up to 25 percent of your trade-show dollars on pre-show invitations is a good
idea.

According to Shelly McKee, vice-president of a management consulting firm that has conducted surveys for the Trade Show Bureau, "You need to do a pre-show telephone invitation—a qualified telephone conversation, saying 'I am excited about this year's show, come see us for these reasons.'"

TIME TIP: *This is the time to test-market new ideas or products that you have had on the back burner. What better time to introduce a product or service to hundreds or thousands of people in a short time? Keep extra invitations next to your phone for new contacts. Now it's four weeks before the show.*

Develop Collateral Material

You can create an inexpensive two-color triple-fold brochure that gives the important points of your business and keep your $4 or $8 brochure to follow up on qualified leads. Even if you have to mail your brochures, there's a cost savings rather than just handing out an expensive brochure to each person who walks by.

TIME TIP: *This is an excellent time to put together clean, simple, and low-budget material for your prospects to receive. Use one sheet per new idea or product. It's now twelve weeks before the show.*

Write Follow-Up Letters Before the Expo

Develop a letter that will be used to say thank-you for stopping by my booth. Personally sign as many letters as you can before the show. If you have developed a special relationship with a participant, write a brief note on a Post-it note and attach it to the letter. You are building your relationship with that person, and you have personalized all the other letters as well with your signature.

TIME TIP: *Keep the letters near your phone, and sign them as you take or make calls.*

Develop a Key Message for Your Exhibit

Every business, including professionals, needs a tag line to use on stationery, business cards, and descriptive literature. I do marketing and public relations and my tag line is "Ideas are only as good as their implementation." Coca-Cola uses "It's the real thing." Seven-up developed "the Uncola." These tag lines reinforce your image with a few words. They subliminally reinforce what you want your customers to remember.

In addition to your tag line, you need a key message for your exhibit. Sometimes your tag line is sufficient, but if you are trying to reach a specific group, then develop a message that speaks to that group. For example, a regional bank had a regular slogan or tag line, but in trying to capture a new audience, it developed a key message on its exhibit: "High Interest for Us—Low Interest to You." They had over 250 inquiries at the show!

Time Tip: Listen to what your customers say about your product or service. Write the comments down—there's an excellent chance your slogan will be there.

Create an Appealing Display

Remember that your booth has less than five seconds to capture someone's attention at a trade show. Michael J. Hatch, president of PEGS Exhibits Inc., in Cheverly, Maryland, recommends a "billboard" approach to booth design: one strong graphic or photo, accompanied by a short, bold headline—preferably one that makes a promise. Don't forget—80 percent of trade show attendees are looking for something *new*. Hatch considers it "one of the most 'sales effective' words you can put on a trade show exhibit."

Another equally strong sales tool is lighting, especially backlit graphics. Large retailers such as Sears Roebuck & Company and Esteé Lauder claim that sales increase as much as sixfold when graphics are backlit rather than frontlit. Why reinvent the wheel? Use their experience for your business.

Create an appealing display by showing an updated business image. If you have used the same exhibit display for the last three to four years, update it. Take advantage of popular new colors and shapes when redoing your display. Use live or video demonstrations, if appropriate. This will draw attendees to your booth and prompt them to ask questions. It also allows you to effectively communicate to a number of prospects at once.

    *TIME TIP: **Changing the lighting to backlit rather than front-lit, or developing new graphics and colors in the display, will update your booth quickly and at low cost.***

    *Time Schedule: **This needs to be done at a minimum of ten weeks before the show.***

Prepare for Market Research

I don't know one business or professional person who is not interested in finding out why customers buy from him or her instead of from the competition, or how customers feel about that person's service or product—what and why they like a particular product or service.

    One service business developed a six-question survey that was used as a qualified-sales lead generator. The income generated from those survey leads surpassed by five times the cost of a booth and collateral material. The owner now is a major sponsor for the event. He swears by the survey as an information and lead generator.

    Some survey questions may be helpful, but limit the number of questions to five or six, or people will be scared off. Have you ever heard about us? What is a major benefit of using our type of product or service? Do you have need for this product or service? And remember to get names, phone numbers, fax numbers, ages, sex, business preferences and needs, and demographic and psychographic information. Think about your business and what you want to know.

    *TIME TIP: **Save thousands of dollars and months of anguish by developing a five- or six-question survey that directly asks what you want to know from customers and prospective clients. It's now eight weeks before the show.***

Prepare General Advertising

Whatever advertising you have planned for the year, add a tag line at the bottom of your current print or radio advertising to say, "See us at Booth 13B at the Business Expo—free drawing for a fax machine."

Print a tag line on your customer's monthly billing statement or print the information on catchy postcards.

TIME TIP: *Make copies of your advertising and pass them out to people at business meetings, appointments, and functions outside the company. Keep a supply in the trunk of your car.*

Decide on Specialty Advertising

Specialty advertising is the give-away gift. The most important thing to remember when developing your specialty advertising campaign is to be *creative* and *useful.* For example, a safety professional gave away two-sided pens—one side had a yellow felt tip and the other a regular blue ink pen. Participants at the show called him to ask for more pens! That is one of the best forms of marketing—people remember who you are and take the time to call you.

Another example of pre-show merchandising is the self-dispensing pencils the stockbroker sent to existing and potential clients. She was overwhelmed with calls. Remember to have fun. As long as the idea is creative and useful, it works as an inexpensive and valuable marketing strategy.

A strategy I developed over the years is to give participants your survey to fill out *before* they get a gift. Most exhibitors also have a drawing for something large—such as a VCR, television, or large food basket. An independent financial advisor gave away a weekend trip to a specific destination.

TIME TIP: *Merchandise your give-aways through pre-show mailings. Send a puzzle piece in your pre-show invitations, and ask prospects to match their piece with the master puzzle in your booth, and receive a prize.*

Train the Staff

The trade show staff must be trained in presenting the product or service you want presented, in trade show etiquette, in how to close a sale, in how to skillfully determine a qualified sales lead, and in the tricks of the trade to keep up energy levels and motivation.

The people you send to the trade show become your CEOs and marketing department; therefore choose and train them wisely. Because of the stiff competition, more and more CEOs, upper management, and technical staff are attending shows and working the booths! For example, Dow Chemical staffed its booth at the National Plastics Show with Ph.D. chemists, the customer-technology contacts of the company. Show participants received the technical or application-specific information rather than a sales pitch. Likewise, at an Association of Operating Room Nurses Show, 3M recognized the position of its Catholic hospital customers and hosted a nonalcoholic hospitality suite.

TIME TIP: Set up appointments with special guests you have invited to the show. Reserve the hospitality room in advance for your VIP visitors. Obtain visitor information for the city where the exposition is taking place, to familiarize your staff with available eating areas and events. It is now four weeks before the show.

Contact the Media

The media are always looking for something new, something modified, something changed. Your press releases must always include a contact person to reach, photos related to the release, and brochures and catalogs that will be distributed at the show. Set up a time for media representatives to see you so you can attend to them individually. When television camera people come to your booth, not only will you get free coverage but you'll also gain attendees.

Send press releases to organizations that you're involved in so mention can be made in their newsletters. Trade journals may use this information as well if you have given them something "new" or presented the information in an interesting way.

If your releases are written before the show, make reprints and distribute them at the show. It makes you look more credible and professional.

TIME TIP: This is the perfect time to get free publicity. Send press releases to the media, including information on new products and services. Make reprints of older articles to hand out at the show. You're now three weeks before the show.

Choose an Appealing Staff Identity

Decide on the image you want to present at the trade show. Do you want your staff to wear suits? Or do you want a theme such as Western, with everyone in Western gear? The staff at a regional conference in San Francisco wore large sombreros with a picture of Golden Gate Park, the bridge, Chinatown, and a cable car. It was not only creative but invited questions.

Sometimes matching blazers or T-shirts identify your staff to prospects who need information or assistance at your booth.

TIME TIP: Brainstorm with employees and customers. Ask them for unique or fun ideas . . . keep them involved.

Gather Show Equipment

Make sure you have your sales literature, order pads, legal pads for names, business cards, a calculator, stapler, masking tape, extension cords, a tool box, and checks or money orders for payments.

TIME TIP: Make plans before the show for an employee, vendor, or friend to check for last-minute glitches and run last-minute errands. It's now one week before the show.

During the Show

It's Show Time!

The show is finally here but the work continues. Conduct daily meetings with your staff to assess the show's progress—what is working and what is not. Process the paperwork, and adjust sales activities and goals if necessary.

You have spent time, money, and energy on your trade show. My marketing strategy for trade shows includes making a favorable impression to existing and prospective clients. Your first impression is made with pre-marketing. Your second is performance at the booth, so it is important to keep aware of booth etiquette:

- *No food.* There is nothing more distracting than watching people eat in their booth. No one wants to disturb you, and that will be disturbing to your final sales.
- *No employee chatting.* Since you have only five seconds to reach an attendee, there is no time for chatting with co-workers. Keep your eye contact on attendees, not employees!
- *No sitting.* Be sure to wear comfortable shoes because you will be standing for several hours, with only short rest intervals. When you stand you are ready to capture what comes your way, and you look sincerely interested in chatting with attendees.
- *Keep up the energy.* Be sure to plan fifteen-minute rest periods every hour for your staff. Encourage them to walk around the show, which gets their circulation going, helps them check out the competition, and increases the likelihood of meeting new people through networking.

After the Show

Send Requested Literature Immediately

The key word here is *immediately.* Send the information you said you would within five working days, if possible. It has the most impact while the trade show is still fresh in everyone's mind. This is the time to send your expensive brochures to your qualified leads.

TIME TIP: *Hire extra help to get your literature out on a timely basis.*

Thank-Yous

This is the time to send the thank-you letters you wrote over three months ago. You have already personalized each letter with your signature.

TIME TIP: Add a Post-it note for "special" contacts. Send these thank-you's within five working days, along with requested literature.

Track Leads Through to the Sale

Track your qualified leads on paper. You will find that if you do many trade shows, a trend will appear. Perhaps in your industry or with your style of selling, the sale will go through after three or five months. Record every qualified customer contact made at the trade show.

Written information will also help you refine your qualified lead sheet for the next trade show.

TIME TIP: Set aside thirty minutes a day, first thing in the morning for follow-up. It helps to clarify and direct your energies. Follow up for one year.

Targeting Business Cards

I like to sort the business cards I collect by location. For example, I live in California, so I gather all the New York business cards under New York, Phoenix business cards under Arizona, and cards from California under specific cities—Los Angeles, San Luis Obispo, San Francisco. This way, when I work with clients in a particular region, I can contact these out-of-state people.

TIME TIP: Put your business card collections in a large binder, separated by state or cities in which you do active business. Do this within two weeks of the show.

Develop a Leads-Source Form

A leads-source form will list your high-priority leads for the next several months. I have developed a leads-source form for my clients that looks like this:

Name	Title	Company	Phone #	Date	Any Information	Source

First Contact	Date	Description
Second Contact		
Third Contact		
Fourth Contact		
Fifth Contact		

Name, title, company name, phone number, date of first contact, any other information you want to record plus the source of your meeting should be listed—"Business Expo. in Wisconsin," for example.

It is very important to record all contacts with your qualified lead, the dates you made them, and a description of what you did—telephone call, sent a note, sent literature, dropped off information, invited the person to a seminar, sent tickets to a ball game, and so on.

TIME TIP: You can combine this record keeping in your database for easy and fast retrieval. Continue this for one full year.

Complete a Critical Evaluation

It is vital that you and the employees who worked at the booth get together and critically evaluate what happened at the show. Did you reach your objectives? What went well and what could have been improved—and *how?* You also need to include questions such as:

Did we reach our target population?
What percentage of attendees did we actually make contact with?
What influence did our booth location have on the impact of our goals?
What were the psychographics of those attendees interested in our product or service?

Did we stay within budget?

You have invested a great deal of money, time, and expense; don't let down at this crucial part of the marketing strategy!

Time Tip: *Spend a few hours* **away** *from your business location (this actually saves time) to discuss these questions and record whatever ideas you come up with. Do this within two weeks of the show. It allows each worker to follow up and digest what went on at the show.*

Summary

Exhibiting at trade shows is an efficient and cost-effective way to reach qualified customers and clients. Select the trade show that will best serve your business interests and those of the customer.

Before the show remember to develop a budget, select appropriate booth features, send out invitations, develop collateral material, write follow-up letters *before* the show, prepare for market research, prepare general advertising, decide on specialty advertising, train the show staff, contact the media, create an appealing display, choose an appealing staff identity, and gather show equipment.

During the show, you want to act and look professional. Therefore: No food eaten inside the booth; no employee chatting; no sitting; and keep your energy up.

After the show, send requested literature immediately, track leads through to the sale, target business cards, send thank-yous, develop the leads-source form, and complete a critical evaluation as to met goals and objectives, what could have been improved, and the type of leads generated. What an excellent opportunity to meet new clients!

Notes

1. Edward A. Chapman, Jr., "Setting Exhibit Goals and Measuring Results," article in the Trade Show Marketing Idea Kit by Skyline™ Displaying Performance.
2. Suzy Banks, "It's Show Time," *Entrepreneurial Woman,* June 1991, p. 71.

12

The Universal Language of Service

We tend to look for more business in all the wrong places: better location, new facility, enlarged facility, increased staff, updated machinery, and increased capital. All these factors may help to increase speed, efficiency, visibility, or image, but they do not make for good business by themselves. The key ingredient is customer service to your existing customers.

Studies show that customers want companies to do what they say they are going to do. They want companies to keep the service promise.

Customer service goes beyond smiles by employees. "Those warm, fuzzy things are certainly part of providing good service, but if customer service were a cake, they'd just be the icing," says Dallas car dealer Carl Sewell, who's been selling through service since 1972. "The real cake would be the systems that allow you to do the job right the first time."[1]

Fran Tarkenton, former NFL quarterback and now CEO of Knowledgeware, Inc., a software company, gave a speech centered on taking care of your customer. After the speech I asked my printer if he had the prices for me on a project and his reply was, "I've been busy in the office all day." I looked at him and asked, "Did you get a chance to listen to Tarkenton's speech?" He said with a wry smile, "I guess I should take care of my present clients." I then asked him, "What am I—chopped liver?"

Michael LeBoeuf, in his book, *How to Win Customers and Keep Them for Life*, says that customers stop doing business with a company because:[2]

1 percent die
3 percent move away
5 percent develop other friendships
9 percent leave for competitive reasons
14 percent are dissatisfied with the product
68 percent quit because of an attitude of indifference toward
   the customer by an employee

Some key factors that make for good customer service include positive attitude, putting your customer's feelings and thoughts before yours, listening to what your customer says and wants, being respectful, and developing creative alternatives to most situations.

For example, a party planner needed thirty kelly-green tablecloths for an event. Rather than call the client and say, "I'm sorry, you will need to change colors," or "No, we do not have them in stock," she came up with a creative idea. She knew the client had centerpieces for the round tables, so she would suggest using tablecloths that had center umbrella holds. This idea of creatively combining regular and umbrella linens made the client happy and the event went extremely well. Customers do not want to know what you can't do for them; they want to know what you *can* do for them.

Customer service is not given only to your direct customers but everyone you do business with, indirectly as well. Everyone is a potential customer. Establishing good customer-service relationships may turn regular customers into representatives for your company, passing on your name to others who may be in a position to use your products or services. They may say positive things about you that others hear, or may change job positions and have cause to use your services in a new way.

Here are some creative customer-service ideas taken from real situations:

- *Flooring company.* Does not have an 800 number, but has a phone number for out-of-town customers to call collect.
- *Graphic artist.* Met a ten-hour deadline on a project even though she had the flu.
- *Food baker.* Sends a package of biscuits as a goodwill gesture to prospective clients.

- *Rabbi.* Calls congregants to wish them well on their birthdays, anniversaries, and so on.
- *Department store.* Employee sends cards to cosmetics purchasers to see if the products worked well.
- *Small boutique.* Calls to tell customers about special sales.
- *School.* Calls parents of new children at the school and checks on their adjustment.
- *Engineering company.* Sends out thank-you notes for attending its open house or other affairs.
- *Insurance agent.* Stays in contact with special clients by dropping off bags of popcorn.
- *Marketing director.* Sends candy to outside support staff.
- *Title company.* Delivers bagels every Friday to its real estate clients.
- *Dentist.* Calls patients at home to see how they are doing after difficult procedures or if they are nervous patients.
- *Decorator.* Sends clippings of articles on arthritis to arthritic clients.
- *Manager.* Brings a large bottle of cranberry juice to a client with kidney stones.
- *Writer.* Sends funny cards with his manuscripts to his editor.
- *Public relations specialist.* Writes a thank-you to media personnel for writing articles or coming to press conferences.
- *Business person.* Shares specialized information with another business person.
- *Party planner.* Freely gives names and phone numbers for related party services.
- *Receptionist.* Answers calls in a cheerful manner, even when she feels overwhelmed by work.
- *Printer.* Sends clients cards or gifts "just because."
- *Computer store.* Calls clients at work to see how they are doing with their new computers.
- *Florist.* Sends a letter to customers announcing a new reminder service for special occasions.

Telephone Talk

Customer service is embodied in an attitude that is reflected on the telephone, through eye contact, in vocal intonation, and posture, and via other types of silent language. Our "talking body parts" are as important as our inventory, bookkeeping, and other basic business operations. Telephone manners and habits are perhaps the most important for good customer service.

The first ten seconds on the phone are the most critical. Therefore, a possible script might be "Thank you for calling [business name]. This is [your name]. How may I help you [serve you or assist you]?"

Because you rely on your sense of hearing when on the phone, it becomes more acute and you pick up nuances rapidly. If I deal with certain people repeatedly, I know just by the way they answer the phone what type of day they're having—if they're stressed, or if they're happy to hear from me.

The telephone can save you time and be a great marketing tool if you use it to your advantage. For example, you want to prevent the following scenario, as shown in Cathy Guisewite's cartoon:

MR. PINKLEY (her boss): "Did you call Peters back for me, Cathy?"

CATHY: "I called Peters back, Mr. Pinkley. He needed some numbers. I made five other calls trying to GET the numbers. No one was in. I got one trainee receptionist, two voice mails and two beeper services. Three of the five called back and left messages while I was trying to fax the request to their fax machines, two of which were out of paper, and one of which was busy for 22 consecutive redials. I finally got one human being who was halfway through giving me the numbers when the battery went dead on his cellular phone and he never called back. I then called four long-lost friends in related businesses, which required four 45-minute catch-up on life chats and obligated me to four two-hour lunches. The friends connected me to an interstate network of contacts, *to whom I now owe 36 follow-up phone calls, 17 notes of appreciation, and 12 permanent entries into our company Christmas card list!!!*"

MR. PINKLEY: ". . . HUH? You called Peters? Great. Will you give Jacobs a call for me when you have a sec?"

Here are some ways to make your telephone your time-saving and marketing friend:

• *Train a screener.* If you have a secretary, an answering service, or an answering machine, you can start the conversation with "Thank you for calling [your company]. How may I serve you?" Every time you use your business name, it is one more time a client or potential client hears the name and you get closer to the eighth "hit."

Have the screener get specific information as to how you can help the caller. In many instances, the caller wants a simple answer of day, time, or where something is to take place. Have your secretary or answering service call back with the requested information.

• *Set a preferred time for calls.* Make a date for the return phone call. This will help eliminate telephone tag. Treat the time as though it were a face-to-face appointment.

• *Group your outgoing calls.* The best times to call back are during the slowest times of your day—usually 11:30 A.M. to noon, and 4:30 to 5:00 P.M. Most people do not want to stay on the phone before lunch or before going home. You may find other slow times in your schedule. Become aware of what those times are and use them to return calls.

• *Make a priority list.* List who needs to be called first, second, and so on. Many times a high-priority call takes care of several lower priority calls.

• *Don't socialize.* Sometimes you hesitate to call someone because the person is long-winded. It's important to let the person know that you are interested in what he or she is saying, but you do not have the time to chat now. For example, "Excuse me, Tom, but I have another appointment in five minutes." Summarize the telephone business and say good-bye.

• *Stand up.* Invest in a fifteen-foot extension cord. Studies have found that you are 17 percent more alert when you're on your feet talking. This is especially helpful during telephone interviews.

Nancy Friedman, owner of The Telephone Doctor, started her business the day she was on the phone to her insurance company and threatened to cancel her policy because of rude telephone treatment. Her agent suggested, "Why don't you come in and talk to my employees about telephone manners?" More than $1 million in sales per year later, Nancy found there is a lot of room for telephone training.

Customer Value Versus Customer Satisfaction

What are some points of *value* for the customer? Saving time, saving money, acknowledgment, follow-up, sticking to quotes and delivery dates, and keeping the customer from looking foolish.

Saving Time

"As I think of the vendors I frequent," comments Jerry, owner of a software company, "I use those companies that save me time. I have only an x amount of time and I need to use it wisely."

Likewise, in my marketing firm, I outsource to several graphics companies. I now use only those that will save me time and deliver the work to my office at no additional cost. One of my favorite graphic artists charges me for delivery, so I rarely use her services. It's important that a business give an impression of value to the customer. This particular artist would be better off charging more for her work and not adding on the delivery fee.

Courier services are popping up all over the country. For a small fee, you can have anything delivered to your clients while you continue to do your work. It's vital that you budget such services into your monthly accounting. They're a small price to pay for the time you save and at the same time you give your customer added value.

A resourceful young man on the East Coast started a business of going to commuter train stations and picking up customer's laundry, then bringing it back to them cleaned either that day or the next day. His business has been brisk, at approximately $1 million a year, because his customers see value in saving time and hassle.

Instead of ordering food to be delivered from only one restaurant, people in some cities can now order an appetizer from one restaurant, the main course from a second one, and dessert from a third, for only a few dollars extra delivery charge. What a value-driven idea that is. For people with tough time schedules, these delivery services offer expanded options.

I send many packages by overnight mail. Rather than take the time to wrap and mail them, I call a mail service that picks up my projects, takes them to a retail office where they are wrapped and weighed, and calls me with the amount of postage. The service will even drop off a roll of stamps if I'm in a pinch for time.

Time is money for all types of businesses. Jim Segers started an accounting practice three years ago. "To keep my costs down," he says, "I use an answering service that knows about my business. When I'm between clients and just don't have time to call someone back, I tell my service to call back and what to say. Many times it's just a time, a date, or a yes or no reply. They charge a few extra cents for this but it saves me a great deal of time. Actually, when I'm under the gun, their services are priceless."

Customers and clients want to feel they received a good deal financially.

John Abrams, a sprinkler mechanic for residential and commercial properties, checks on new and repaired sprinklers he's installed for sixty days after the work is completed. "My business has grown from word of mouth," he says.

A printing company offers free color (red) on all printing one day a week. Customers feel they are saving money on two-color print runs as a result.

A latte and cappuccino coffee shop that predominantly sells coffee offers a coffee card to all of their customers. After eight coffee visits, they receive their ninth free.

Demonstrations are excellent ways to give your customer more value. An arts supply and party shop provides on-going demonstrations in the store on ways to assemble and make projects. The customer feels he is saving money by buying the pieces to make the project, or has had a lesson on how to do it, and feels a sense of accomplishment when the project is completed. Breis Stone, the store manager, says, "We have a very high repeat customer base. The demonstrations play a large role in our customer service efforts."

I frequent a particular restaurant often. I like going there for business meetings because they always acknowledge my presence very professionally. It adds professional credibility to my lunch partners.

Ken and Linda Sanders, owners of an engineering firm, repeatedly take their clients out to a particular restaurant because, "We are very well taken care of by the waiters and the maitre d'. They acknowledge us as their special guests, and I know I'll always get the bill handed to me," says Ken.

Saving Money

A client of mine, Linda Rutgers, recently bought a second-hand computer. The person who sold her the equipment was available to set it up, exchange files, and do anything else she required. "Even though I feel I paid about $200 too much for the computer, I received much more than that in added value," Linda claims.

Providing Acknowledgment

Everyone wants to feel special and acknowledged, especially in business situations. You want to give your customers and clients an impression of authority, credibility, or professionalism. Restaurants are a perfect place for such acknowledgment.

Giving Follow-Up

True marketing starts when you've made the sale. Follow-up during the sale is paramount, but follow-up after the sale is even more important. For example, a large apparel manufacturing company responds directly to each complaint it receives. The company received a complaint about unraveling buttonholes on a particular dress. Customer service wrote back stating that "Loose buttons or imperfect buttonholes are unacceptable," with instructions to have the dress altered by a tailor and the company would reimburse the customer. Just an aside: the dress had been well worn and was not expensive. That's follow-up.

Good follow-up leads to additional sales, but the opposite is also true. I bought a super typewriter at a local business over eight years ago. The salesperson made "office calls" whenever my secretary did not understand something on the machine. I was pleased with the service and bought an expensive copier two years later. Six years after that, I bought another copier at the same business and had nothing but nightmarish follow-up. To get the owner's attention (since he did not return my calls), I sent my letters certified. The cost to that company for their no service or follow-up was over $3,000 I spent on a new computer, purchased elsewhere.

A California manufacturer of natural foods was displeased to receive a letter commenting on the shortage of raisins in its cereal boxes. The company's president not only thanked the person for writing the letter but sent a replacement box of cereal, two other products in the line, coupons for more purchases, a questionnaire about the enclosed products, a postcard to give to retailers requesting they carry the product, and a statement that explained how the products help in lowering cholesterol.

Companies need to take the time initially when projecting bids and delivery dates to their customers. It's important to stay timely and on target.

Sticking to Quotes and Delivery Dates

One company won a bid on a residential air-conditioner and budgeted $100 for installation with a crane. "On the day we were supposed to do the work, the ground was too wet to get the crane in, and there was no asphalt to drive it near the house. But since we had promised the customer we'd complete the job that same day, we hired a helicopter for $500."

The air-conditioner was installed during the rain and fog,

and the work was videotaped. The customer offered to split the extra $400 but the company would not accept. "Well, that customer showed the videotape at his New Year's Eve party, and we got three new leads and one sale from that. The sale was a five-ton unit, and our profit was $2,400. So for an initial $400 investment in customer service, we figure, our return was 600 percent."

The customers or clients must never feel that you have blamed them for a mistake nor feel foolish for doing or saying something.

Keeping the Customer From Looking Foolish

A large executive-search agency in the health-care industry strongly believes in keeping the customer happy and giving added value. Sharon Gross says, "The chairman of a client company called me on a Sunday morning to complain that our candidate for a position failed to show up for a board meeting that day. Even though I knew that the client was wrong, that the candidate wasn't due until the following Sunday, I took the blame for the mistake, apologizing profusely and asking if my candidate could appear at a later date.

"Grudgingly, the chairman agreed to reschedule. Because I refused to turn the error into a 'his fault/our fault' dispute, we maintained the customer relationship. If I'd made the chairman look foolish in front of his board by insisting that he was at fault, there's no doubt in my mind that he would have fired us from the search." A few days later the chairman did call to admit that he made a mistake.

Customer Service Needs to Be Proactive

In the old days, customer service was down the hall in "that" department and usually consisted of complaints that got a reactive focus. Sales representatives did not take care of the problem; it was sent to customer service or, more precisely, the customer complaint department.

Today's competitive climate urges small-business owners to

take a proactive focus on customer service. It's time to throw out the specialized department of complaints, where only a few people take responsibility for the problems. Rather, a proactive focus includes such services as:

- *Use of technology.* Checking the computerized inventory to determine if a replacement item is in stock and when it will be delivered.
- *Total customer quality.* Training and empowering sales people to help customers with further directions. The salesperson's role is to make sure the customer is satisfied.
- *Total customer follow-up.* Keeping in touch with the customer. You drop a note to each customer saying thank-you for the purchase and ask how the product is working out.

This is the beauty of small business; you are small enough to give customer service in a timely manner. Personal attention in most large companies is lost in the maze of paperwork or redtape.

Six Service Strategies That Work

1. *Make it easy for customers to do business with you.* Customers want things fast and easy. The easier you make it, the better the response will be. For example, in direct marketing you have a better chance of getting a response if you include a reply card. Customer intentions are good, but customers get busy and forget. Businesses that have hotlines to take care of questions and offer support help make it easier for the consumer.

2. *Turn complaints into repeat business.* Look at a complaint as a sales opportunity. You get a chance to speak to the customer one-on-one. If the customer is handled well during the complaint, loyalty will be stronger than if there were no complaint in the first place. It is important to handle the complaint well and handle it quickly.

Studies have shown that it is five to six times more expensive and time-consuming to attract one new customer than to keep your existing customers happy. It is also estimated that it takes twelve years to get back old customers once you have lost them.

Nordstrom's Department Store is a classic example of taking

care of complaints. A woman bought a blouse there over two years ago but never wore it, and did not have the sales slip, yet was able to return the blouse without explanation. Jim and Bruce Nordstrom have said, "97 percent of our customers are good and solid. Only 3 percent of our customers abuse our policy."

A good way to turn a complaint into a loyal customer is to ask "What can I do to make it right by you?" You will be surprised by the comments. Customers usually want less from you than you're willing to give.

3. *Make your customer feel safe.* Many newsletter subscriptions have a money-back guarantee. In other words, you can order the newsletter or journal and if you don't like it, you get your money back without questions. The customer feels safe; there is no perceived risk.

I do a great deal of business with a particular graphic artist because she makes my clients feel safe. She puts together a couple of logo designs for my clients and charges only for what they like. If they don't like any of them, she goes back to the drawing board. It's a safe relationship for me because I don't have to pay for the extra time. If the client decides not to go with any of the designs, there is no cost incurred. This artist's business has grown by 50 percent in the last eighteen months.

Sample-size products are another way to give the customer perceived safety. Cosmetics can be expensive, but what happens if you buy them and you don't like them or you're allergic to them? Sample-size products solve this dilemma.

Service companies can also give "samples" of their service. Donating one hour of professional service for a local fund-raiser not only gets your name out to the community but also gives prospective clients an opportunity to sample your work. I recently donated one hour of my marketing services, working with an auction winner for one hour. She attended two of my seminars and is now a client.

4. *Wow your customer.* The other morning I went to a gas station convenience store for some "emergency" milk. I was told by the woman behind the counter that there was a price reduction on the one-gallon milk cartons. I returned my quart in place of the gallon. She also suggested that I try a cup of the store's gourmet

coffee and fill out a few questions on a survey. I was impressed not only with the minimum-wage-earner's degree of customer service but also with the fact that the store went through the trouble and expense of serving that gourmet coffee.

There's a small coffeehouse in northern California that my husband and I love to visit. The place has a huge selection of magazines and newspapers. Customers buy their beverage, food, or newspaper and read any magazine on display, then return it to the stand. We're usually there for hours, sifting through magazines, buying only a fraction of what we enjoy there.

5. *Find a solution for your customer.* Don't say no. Your customers and clients come to you to solve a problem or fill a need. The worst word you can say is *no.* For example, "No, we don't carry that." "No, we're out." "No, I don't work in this department." The above may all be true, but you don't want to use the word *No,* for two reasons: (1) when people hear "no," that's what they remember and they stop listening for a while because they feel lost at that moment; and (2) using "no" starts your relationship with customers on a negative note. They don't want to know what you *can't* do for them; they want to know what you *can* do—that's why they're there in the first place.

A positive response may be that *you're out of the item:* "Let me show you what we do have." "What do you need this item for?" "How are you going to use this item?" Suggest an alternative way or another item that will solve the problem. "I'd be happy to special order this for you." "I'd be happy to call our other stores for you."

Another response is to say *you've never stocked the item.* Start a regular conversation with the customer and then ask, "What do you need this item for?" You can suggest something that you do have in stock and will work.

Or what if *you've never provided the service?* You have a choice: You can refer the client or customer to someone you know who does the requested service, or you can accept the challenge of providing the service yourself. Do the latter if you feel confident that you have the knowledge and experienced backup people to call on.

6. *Stay positive.* We have approximately 50,000 thoughts a day, of which 80 percent are negative. How do you turn the majority of

negative thoughts into positive ones? By saying positive self-talk statements—"This is a good day." "I am productive." And smile, even when you don't feel like it. Others will respond to you. When you smile, others will smile back and you'll begin to feel more positive as the day goes along. When you're positive, you listen better and want to help customers.

I recently felt like having ice cream on a rainy, humid day. I didn't think many people would be at the ice cream parlor. Well, there was a line of four people waiting and only one server. The server was in the back putting together some ice cream cakes. Twenty minutes later I had my one scoop of ice cream. Throughout all this tension, the server kept smiling and apologizing for our having to wait. We weren't happy about waiting, but her smile dissolved any anger we had.

How's Your Customer Service?

Carl Sewell, the country's top luxury-car dealer in Dallas, Texas, developed the Ten Commandments of Customer Service in his book, *Customers for Life*.[3] These commandments are:

> 1. Bring 'em back alive. Ask customers what they want and give it to them again and again.
> 2. Systems, not smiles. Saying please and thank you doesn't insure you'll do the job right the first time, every time. Only systems guarantee you that.
> 3. *Underpromise, overdeliver.* Customers expect you to keep your word. Exceed it.
> 4. When the customer asks, the answer is always yes. Period.
> 5. Fire your inspectors and consumer relations department. Every employee who deals with clients must have the authority to handle complaints.
> 6. No complaints? Something's wrong. Encourage your customers to tell you what you're doing wrong.
> 7. Measure everything. Baseball teams do it. Football teams do it. Basketball teams do it. You should, too.

8. Salaries are unfair. Pay people like partners.

9. Your mother was right. Show people respect. Be polite. It works.

10. Japanese them. Learn how the best really do it; make their systems your own. Then improve them.

Carl Sewell's warning is: "These ten rules aren't worth a damn . . . unless you make a profit. You have to make money to stay in business and provide good service."[4]

Summary

Key factors that make for good customer service include a positive attitude, putting your customer's feelings and thoughts before yours, listening to what your customer says and wants, being respectful, and developing creative alternatives to most situations.

Customer service also includes good telephone skills. Six ways to use the telephone as your business partner are to train a screener, set a preferred time to return calls, group your outgoing calls during the slowest times of your day, make a priority list of calls, don't socialize on the phone, and stand up while talking on the phone.

Customer value exceeds customer satisfaction. Saving time, saving money, providing acknowledgment, giving follow-up after the sale, sticking to quotes and delivery dates, and keeping the customer from looking foolish are points of value for your customers and clients.

Customer service needs to be proactive by giving each employee the responsibility of "making the sale work." Six successful service strategies are to make it easy for customers to do business with you, turn complaints into repeat business, make your customer feel safe, wow your customer, find a solution for your customer, and stay positive.

Notes

1. Carl Sewell, *Customers for Life: How to Turn That One-Time Buyer Into a Lifetime Customer* (New York: Doubleday, 1990). Copyright © 1990 by

Carl Sewell. Used by permission of Doubleday, a division of Bantam Doubleday Dell Publishing Group, Inc.

2. Michael LeBoeuf, *How to Win Customers and Keep Them for Life* (New York: Putnam, 1987).

3. Sewell, op. cit. Copyright © 1990 by Carl Sewell. Used by permission of Doubleday, a division of Bantam Doubleday Dell Publishing Group, Inc.

4. Ibid.

13
Creating an Image

Do your customers know who *you* are along with the services and products you provide? What is the image you are trying to portray? Your image determines how you and your business are perceived by others. Research has shown that the closer you are to your clients or customers in attitudes, values, interests, and background, the more attractive they perceive you. How do you package the person you are and what your business is? You need to think of your business in terms of What? Who? and How? *What* does your business do and how can this solve your customer's needs and problems? *Who* is your targeted group? *How* is your business different and better than your competition? Let's look at an example of this:

- *What.* Mike Danes, a safety and claims consultant, works with companies to develop safer work habits for their employees as well as helps employers lower their workers compensation claims. The safety and claims information and the education he provides save employees from possible physical problems and save employers from potential lawsuits.
- *Who.* Targeted client groups include any business whose employees have the possibility of getting hurt on the job or where a violent act might be committed. The targeted groups include oil-related companies, hospitals, convenience stores, and hotels.
- *How.* The business is unique, in that Mike does not try to be all things to all business. He focuses on safety, claims, and violence in the workplace. He keeps current with federal and state regulations. In fact, he wrote a workbook and gives seminars, including at various institutions such as the local state university.

Seven Ways to Sell Yourself

Realize that everyone is selling something—ideas, products, or services. With that in mind, it is easy to understand why you need to sell yourself first, before you sell your idea, product, or service.

1. *Become knowledgeable in what you're trying to sell.* Customers like dealing with people who are knowledgeable about the product or service they're interested in buying. You feel more comfortable when the person selling you something knows everything that's important to know. It helps make your decision easier, because the salesperson reinforces what you find important and useful.

TIME TIP: Hold weekly meetings with your employees. Together, brainstorm new marketing ideas and determine how to become a resource for education on your products and services. Bring in motivational speakers or the vendors for a product, and exchange selling expertise. This saves time by eliminating costly errors "because someone didn't know how to do something." You can't assume that employees know how to market the business.

2. *Really believe in what you are selling.* For years I have said at seminars, in speeches, and at meetings with clients that you must really believe in what you are selling. If you don't believe in nuclear power plants, then you must get out of a job that sells those plants. If you don't like answering machines, then don't sell them.

Business owners for years have known that if employees do not like a certain piece of inventory, that piece becomes much more difficult to move. Business owners usually put a slow-moving item on sale or give employees an incentive—usually a monetary bonus. My father immigrated to America after World War II and found himself selling shoes in a department store. The majority of his salary came from PMs (promotional merchandise) because he really believed in the incentive!

Booksellers and book reps help make books bestsellers. This is exactly what happened with Robert James Waller's *The Bridges of Madison County.* The reviews were not positive, but sales reps read the book and loved it. They suggested that booksellers carry it in their stores. Booksellers read it and loved it, suggesting the title to their customers. Customers suggested the book to their friends.

Build a relationship with your vendors and keep lines of communication open. Let them know when their suggestions work and when they don't. The vendor that is in business for the long run will be honest with you.

TIME TIP: Get your employees involved in purchasing. You will find that the items your employees suggest buying are usually the ones that do best—not because they are the nicest or the best but because they are suggested and "hand sold."

TIME TIP: Be sure you enjoy and believe in what you're selling. It saves time and a great deal of stress to choose your job or career carefully. If you don't love what you do, then make changes as soon as possible. Most of your waking hours are spent working.

3. *Show how what you're selling meets the buyer's needs and wants.* There are two good ways to find out what your clients need or want: (1) ask them, and (2) listen to what they say and what they imply. More times than not, customers will tell you what they want.

Communicating what your idea, product, or service can do for the customer helps solve the buyer's dilemma or confusion. Helping customers make good buying decisions for themselves or their families turns you into a hero. They appreciate your help and chances are good that they will come back for your help again in the future. This is true whether you're selling automobiles, appliances, accounting, or research data.

TIME TIP: It saves time to know what your client wants the first time around, rather than guess at it or find out later. Listen to what your client says. Ask open-ended questions (those questions that cannot be answered by a yes or no response). Good words to start with are **What** *and* **How.** *Stay away from first words like* **Is** *or* **Did?**

4. *What you say should be consistent with how you say it.* Your body language is a true mirror of how you feel about something.

In fact, how you say something is more believable than what you say, if the two are not consistent.

Many years ago I took skiing lessons. On the first morning, I learned how to go down a bunny slope. My husband shouted from the bottom of the hill to relax. I yelled back that I was relaxed, as I descended the hill tense and muscles cramping.

What about employees who ask the customer, "How are you doing this morning?" while they totally ignore the answer? Recently I was with a group of adults at a coffeehouse, sitting on the patio near about eight other tables of people. All of a sudden extra-loud music came over the speakers. I went in to ask an employee to lower the noise, and the employee nodded her head that she would. As I went outside again I noticed another employee quickly stacking the chairs. I asked if he was closing, and he gave a timid nod with his head. A few minutes later, everyone left. The next morning I returned to the coffeehouse, for two reasons: it served freshly squeezed orange juice and I just had to ask the manager if that was how they consistently asked customers to leave. The manager was astonished that his staff had acted in this manner and said he would speak to them. I received my orange juice free for the inconvenience.

I am trying to adopt a healthier lifestyle, which includes taking vitamins. I went to a well-known iridologist (a person who looks into the iris for indications of bodily health and disease). The man was extremely knowledgeable, but spoke so quickly that it appeared to be rote repetition. I don't have confidence that his recommendations will work, because he is overweight and extremely disorganized. There was an inconsistency between what he said and how he looked.

TIME TIP: Be careful to take the time to be consistent in what and how you say something. Take the time to remember that each person is different and reads your body language as well as what you say. By taking the time to be consistent, you've earned a new client.

5. *Dress appropriately for what you are selling.* Very few people get away with dressing inappropriately at their jobs or in their careers. Most people expect attorneys to wear a suit and tie while at

the office and lab technicians to wear white lab coats (although many opt for softer pastel colors).

I have a client who does landscaping and gardening. For a publicity photo, he brought a collared and buttoned shirt and a nice T-shirt printed with his business name. We decided it was more appropriate for him to wear his T-shirt because that's how his clients saw him most of the time.

Another client, Mike Jacobs, had his picture taken for a flyer and brought along a tie. This was the first time I had seen him with a tie. We decided to take his picture with a collared shirt and sports jacket instead—the way he looks when he works with his clients. Much of what he does is hands-on, and he gets pretty dirty at times.

TIME TIP: Use the trunk of your car as a wardrobe enhancer. The landscaping client would do well to have a clean T-shirt in the trunk when he wants to approach new customers. He also needs to have a brown and blue tie in his car at all times so he can easily don it for those times when he needs it.

It's also a good idea for men to have an extra clean shirt at the office, and women to have a few extra pairs of pantyhose and low-heeled or pump shoes for dressier events.

6. *Be enthusiastic about what you are selling.* Nothing seems as contagious in business as enthusiasm—enthusiasm in selling, in providing service, and in follow-up. Enthusiasm about what you do gives customers the feeling that you really believe what you say and you care about them personally.

Try to use as many services or products as you sell, giving first-hand knowledge of how they work as well as their quirks.

TIME TIP: Take the time to learn more about your products or service and share this new knowledge with the customer. Establish yourself as an "expert," or at least a very knowledgeable person in this area, and your income generally reflects this.

7. *Passionately believe that what you are selling helps the buyer in some way.* One client shares an example of his business passion: "I

can work on someone's skin to make it healthier and watch my client become more confident with herself."

When I had my clothing boutique, I believed that the items we sold in the store were of great value. I constantly told my customers that they would tire of the clothes before they wore out. In addition, I truly believed the way our fashion consultants put items together for clients made a big difference in their outlooks. After all, some of the clothes could easily have been bought at competitors' stores. Our store culture was to give the customer the best look and quality for the money. When women wore clothes from the store, they almost always were complimented on the way they looked.

An accounting client came up with a way to help a financially strapped small business with cash flow. As we've mentioned many times before, it takes less time to keep an existing client than it does to find a new one. The small business recommended the accountant to a multimillion dollar business, resulting in a lucrative account.

TIME TIP: Brainstorm ways you can help certain clients. More times than not, by passionately helping your clients and customers they in turn become your best marketing representatives.

Build Your Business Image

There are several inexpensive and time-saving ways to build a strong business image. Let's look at a few of these ideas.

A Mission Statement With Meaning

Think of the vision for your business as a "dream list" and your mission statement as the strategy for realizing your dreams. By incorporating a dream list you develop a mission statement with meaning. It no longer is idle words.

One of my clients, a management consultant, was having some problems staying focused on what she wanted to do in her consulting business. She listed what she wanted to do with her business, then turned her three top-priority items into a mission statement. The following is an example of what we developed:

Her vision: "I want to write books, create audios, give speeches, develop weekly programs, get an existing book published, and facilitate and present seminars."

Her three top-priority items were:

Give speeches
Develop weekly programs
Write books

Her mission statement: "To work with people in setting the path for health and stress prevention by presenting speeches, weekly programs, and writing books that offer ways to make people's lives more prosperous, positive, and action-driven."

One of the best mission statements ever was devised by NASA during the 1960s. It was simple, but created tremendous activity and commitment: "We're going to put a man on the moon."

Personal Bios

Every business owner and his or her employees must have biographical information ready to send out when needed and easily updated as circumstances change. The business bio is an important marketing tool.

> TIME TIP: *Have a get-together of your staff every six months to update your company bio, the owner's bio, and a bio for each employee. This not only saves time but the end products are better thought out and more representative of the business.*

Use a brainstorming session to help each person write his or her bio. Share mutual information, because it's difficult for most people to write their own bios. I asked my husband to write my bio for the jacket of my first book. The publisher expanded it from there.

Sometimes it's difficult to know where to start, but you will want to include these items:

Complete name (including middle initial or "Jr.")
Your business title
How long you have been working in the area
Your certifications or degrees
Any recent awards or scholarships
Personal data such as married, three children
Where you moved from and when
A few related jobs or titles and dates
A brief description of what you do
Mention of any articles or media attention
Club or society memberships

Presently I am working with a client to put together a seminar with eight speakers from different disciplines. I was impressed with three of the eight biographies sent by the speakers. In other words, I would use the services only of the three business people whose biographies told me they were professional, organized, and good at what they did. One potential speaker's biography—a marriage, family, and child counselor—was hand scribbled, messy, and boring.

I was most impressed with the following biography, which was printed on the person's business stationery:

Roland H. Brown, Jr., Owner of Babe's Gym, has been a professional personal fitness trainer since 1984. His expertise in physical fitness comes originally from an extensive background in dance and body movement. He studied dance at the University of Texas in Austin, and was a professional dancer for ten years. After becoming a certified aerobics instructor in 1983, Roland moved into bodybuilding, placing in two AC-BCC-sanctioned amateur body-building competitions in 1987: Mr. Los Angeles Natural and Mr. California Natural.

Roland began his personal training career in Los Angeles in 1984, and has since designed and implemented literally hundreds of personalized programs for clients utilizing a balance of cardiovascular exercise, strength training, flexibility and postural enhancement.

Roland and his wife, Darla, a Bakersfield native, moved to Bakersfield in May 1990, where he began training clients out of the Phase I Fitness facility. In January 1991, he opened the Roland and Associates Personal Fitness Training studio on Bernard Street so that his clients would have more privacy, more personalized attention, and fewer distractions than they had at a "public" club. In only a 19-month period, it became clear that the business had again "outgrown" its facility. So in August 1992, he opened The Fitness Solution on Westwind Drive. In May 1994, the Browns purchased Bakersfield's historic Babe's Gym, which offers memberships and serves as a private training facility.

Since arriving in Bakersfield in May 1990, Roland has been featured in five articles in *The Bakersfield Californian,* and has appeared on several local news segments on television.

Roland is a member in good standing of the American College of Sports Medicine (ACSM), the National Strength and Conditioning Association (NSCA), and the IDEA Association for Fitness Professionals. He is also an active member of the Greater Bakersfield Chamber of Commerce, the Bakersfield Rotary Club, the Executives Association of Kern County, and the Downtown Business Association.

Mascot or Personal Trademark

A husband-and-wife realtor team is approaching $10 million in sales, in a market-driven field where the median price for a residential house is $95,000. They have developed a personal marketing image using their one-pound pet fennec fox (the smallest fox in the world), named Prudence. The husband says, "We needed something to set us apart from the more than 1,200 sales associates in our area. Prudence was it." He goes on to say, "You need an identity. I'm not saying that every one should get a fox for a mascot, but think about your identity . . . think about personal marketing. In today's market it is critical. Every sales associate needs an identity. For us, it's Prudence. For someone else, who knows? But it works."

A successful national speaker on motivation, Patricia Fripp, wore incredible hats as her trademark. She felt she needed to stand out from the crowd and her large, fancy, and impressive hats made that happen.

Jay Leno, the network talk-show host, uses his chin as his trademark. It's difficult to find a sketch or an article that does not in some way show or mention his distinguishing feature.

An entrepreneur who owns a popcorn and gift franchise, Karen Cann, uses red and white colors. She wears predominantly red clothing: red tennis shoes, red dresses, and red shorts. She even had her car repainted red, and bought a personalized license plate.

In other words, develop a mascot or trademark to go along with your personal image, or enhance an existing feature such as Leno's chin or Paul Newman's baby-blue eyes.

Your Handshake

Handshakes tell people a lot about your level of confidence. A strong handshake normally means you are confident, while a limp one makes you perceived as nonassertive and passive. It is just as important for women to have an assertive handshake as it is for men.

A California sales manager developed the following eight handshake theories when he was a psychology student, and he has perfected them as a salesperson over the last twenty years. They tell a lot about you or the person you are shaking hands with.

> *The All-American.* This person looks you in the eyes, smiles, and shakes several times. The handshake delivers a feeling of relaxed self-confidence. It is hearty and genuine.
>
> *The Push-Off.* The grip can be warm, but at the end the hand is flicked away. This shake implies the need to establish territory. This person is not interested in what you have to say. You leave the handshake feeling rebuffed.
>
> *The Pull-In.* This is the opposite of the push-off. This person holds onto your hand and guides you in a direction. The shake could pull you toward the handshaker or direct you through a door or to a chair. A handshake like this is a good sign the person is maneuvering you.
>
> *Two-Handed.* The right hand grabs yours. The left

hand manipulates, pushing, pulling, directing. A hand clasped around this way connotes intimacy or ownership.

The Finger Squeeze. The finger-squeeze is used to keep someone at a distance. There is nothing warm or inviting about it. On the extreme end is the bone crusher—an insecure person who equates brute strength with personal power.

The Palm Pinch. This person offers two, maybe three fingers. It is typically delivered by someone who hasn't learned to shake hands or has a fear of engagement. No energy transfer occurs.

The Water Well. This person shakes your hand like he or she is drawing water from a well. The initial good feeling evaporates after the fourth or fifth shake.

The Dead Fish. This person doesn't muster the energy or interest to give you a real handshake. It is dead, cold, clammy, and indifferent. This individual is a passive person with little self-esteem.

Dressing for Impact

How you dress *does* make a difference. It may not be fair, but it is a fact when it comes to business. John T. Molloy, author of *The New Dress for Success,* says "You know who comes to us? CEOs, the highest earning sales people, politicians. Over decades of consulting, I've learned that the more sophisticated a person is, the more he or she is interested in image."[1]

Follow the direction of your boss. In some companies, a dressed-down look is appropriate and in others the suit is most appropriate. A few things to remember are to keep your clothes cleaned and looking fresh and your shoes clear of heel marks. For women, go easy on the fragrances, jewelry, and makeup. Those first few seconds do count.

Body Language

As discussed earlier in the chapter, how you communicate is usually more believable than what you say. The cliché "Words are worth a dime a dozen" does hold true. Actions speak louder than words in most instances. Let's look at what might account for the discrepancy between what and how something is said.

Eye Contact

Your eye contact is possibly the most important type of body language. We are brought up to believe that if you're telling the truth, then you look squarely in the other person's eyes as you speak. If you look down, we believe that something is not right. However, this is not the case in some other cultures. It may be rude to look directly at someone when speaking. It is important to understand eye contact within the culture you are working.

Voice Inflection

Have you noticed that when you get angry or frightened, your voice may quiver and get higher and louder? Most of us are unaware of inflection, and yet this piece of body language is rapidly picked up by others. Boring lectures happen when the speaker maintains the same tone of voice; after a while, that monotone puts listeners to sleep. On the other hand, speakers are interesting when they vary their voice from a higher pitch to a lower one. Voice inflection picks up our motivation and enthusiasm on a topic or can show how uninterested we are.

Posture

Many doctors feel that one reason why so many people suffer back problems is their posture—or more specifically, lack of posture. Spending hours at your desk, at the computer, and in other necessary positions tends to give your muscles the wrong message. Learn to stretch, do yoga, or learn martial arts to straighten your muscles and give your body the signal to keep working properly.

Jerking Movements

I have observed that when someone is uncomfortable with a topic, he or she tends to fidget, change sitting positions, scratch the head, rub the eye, and do other "jerking" movements. When these movements occur during interviews, ask questions that will get you an idea of who the other person really is.

Personal Introductions

Marjorie Brody, a business etiquette expert in Elkins Park, Pennsylvania, says, "Etiquette is simple, which makes it all the more unforgivable not to know it."

When you are introduced to someone new, don't botch it. The rule of thumb in personal introductions is to introduce the authority figure or person in the highest position first. When introducing a customer to an employee or vendor, introduce the client first: "Ms. James, I'd like you to meet the head of purchasing, Mr. Sand."

Table and Telephone Manners

The good news is that table manners can be learned, since many of us have not had good role models. An etiquette expert in California observed that there are three generations that have not had proper role models for personal or business etiquette: the baby-bust generation, the baby-boom generation, and generation X. She feels that parents and grandparents have not taught children proper etiquette. She goes on to say that we learn by watching others, who do not necessarily know what they are doing. The niceties notwithstanding, the most important thing to remember is to use your utensils.

There are a few important points to remember about telephone etiquette. Say good morning or afternoon, introduce yourself, and give the name of your business. This gives the caller or receiver a chance to identify whom they are speaking with. Introducing yourself in this way is also an important marketing tool. And an occasional "thank you" and "please" sprinkled throughout the conversation are also effective telephone etiquette. People like to be acknowledged, and saying thank you is one way to do this.

Professional Marketing Tools

Slogans

What is your slogan? What comments do you hear your customers say about you and your business? Almost all larger companies have some type of slogan. For example, can you remember where you've heard the following? The answers follow:

"Where Customer Service is State of the Art"
"The Uncola"
"The Real Thing"
"Choice of a new generation"

ANSWERS: Circuit City, 7-Up, Coke, Pepsi-Cola.

Cards, Stationery, Logos

Do your cards and stationery reaffirm your business image? Is your card on heavy stock, easy to read, in two or three colors? I received a letter from someone the other day. I was impressed with what the person had to say until I came to the business card. The address had been crossed out and handwritten with the new one. In addition, there was too much information on the business card and it looked crowded. The card seemed inconsistent with the person's business image as a financial planner!

Kmart Corporation developed a new logo several years ago, especially important since this large retailer wanted to change its image as the "polyester palace." Kmart announced plans that it was going to spend $2.3 billion during the next five years to give its stores a facelift and fresher look. Kmart Chairman Joseph Antonini said at the time, "We want our retail identity to represent what Kmart is about today. This new symbol keeps Kmart in step with the times and reflects the dynamism and excitement of the company's commitment to renewal."

TIME TIP: When developing or changing your business identity, keep your systems consistent—business cards, stationery, envelopes, and address labels. Never cross anything out before handing it to a client or customer. Order new cards and envelopes when there is any change in information. Winning the confidence of one new customer will more than pay for the printing.

Brochures

What type of image do you want to project in your brochure? Who is your target audience? Do you have more than one target? You may want one or a combination of these image themes brought out:

Credibility
Longevity in business or in the field
Honesty
Size of the business
Humorous, easy-going hometown feeling
Experience

Your brochure is your silent marketing representative or salesperson. It not only describes your products or services when you're not around but also gives the person reading it the push to call you. Keep the following ideas in mind when developing your brochure:

▪ *What is your goal in producing the brochure?* Why are you spending time and money to develop it? Your purpose might be to upgrade your product's or company's image, or to describe new services or products.

▪ *Who is your target audience?* If the brochure is for manufacturers or wholesalers, it should be straightforward. If your target is a conservative group, it needs to be conservative in look and feel. If you're aiming at the general consumer, it may need quite a bit of color and dazzle.

For example, a client wanted to introduce a dessert cobbler. We had to decide who the target market was—that would tell us what type of packaging we needed. We decided to go after the wholesale trade—restaurants. The packaging was straightforward, simple, and functional. If we had chosen supermarkets as the target group, the packaging would have been colorful and special looking.

• *What are the audience's buying motives?* Always write your copy with your customer's point of view in mind. Stress the ways your product or service can fill their needs—how your products or services will benefit them. There's a difference between features and benefits. Benefits, not features, sell a product or service:

Cars   Feature: big, shiny
              Benefit: makes you look successful

Real estate   Feature: three bedrooms and a living room
              Benefit: house with a family feeling and spacious
                  room for entertaining friends and family

Law   Feature: estate planning
              Benefit: help you save money and plan for the
                  future

• *What is the theme of your brochure?* Blend theme and graphic design. If your audience is health minded, you may want to use a theme of fitness, exercise, and freshness. The design should reinforce the image or identity of your company, product, or service.

TIME TIP: *If you're not an expert with computer design, delegate this task to a graphic artist or printing business with creative designers. Not only will the finished product look more professional but you will have saved yourself hours of exhaustive labor when you could have been creating something new for your business or marketing a new idea to your clients.*

• *How will you organize what you want to say?* The front cover is used to introduce yourself, with your name or the name of your business. Then include an important benefit. On the back cover, repeat your name or name of your business, plus your address, phone number, and fax number, if you have one. Use large, bold headlines inside. Organize the headlines into four to six key elements or areas, with benefits listed for each. Use subheadings to tell the story or sell the message.

• *What kind of paper will you use?* The type of paper you use is important to the overall image you want to project. If your business is health, fitness, or environmental consciousness, then use recycled paper. If your business is more conservative—finance, banking, law, or engineering—you may want to use white glossy paper. When in doubt, spend the extra few cents and get what you want.

Time Tip: When developing your brochure, find creative ways to direct the brochure to several target audiences. This will not only save you time but also money. Unattached inserts work well for this.

Newsletters

Newsletters are a great way to keep in contact with your customers. But there is no way a business with hundreds or thousands of clients can keep in touch with each client without using a communication vehicle. That communication vehicle is the newsletter.

An attorney with 1,800 people in his database was having a difficult time keeping in touch. It was causing him increasing frustration, and as a result his database was not increasing. We developed a quarterly newsletter. The image of the newsletter was credibility, humor (the client is a joke teller), and information. Through this communication vehicle, he had an easy, cost-effective, and time-efficient way to market his seminars and three major areas of legal practice. The attorney consistently receives calls from people who have received his newsletter, and they compliment him on the look or content.

Enhance Your Image

If yours is a very small business, give the impression that you're much larger than you really are. In other words, you can handle not only a variety of tasks but a quantity of them as well. This is especially helpful for the small-business owner and people in home-based businesses.

For example, in the early 1980s, a young divorced mother left her job at a large computer company and started her own business developing software. Her first client was her old employer. She built up her company and successfully sold it within ten years to a large corporation. She often tells about how she gave the impression of being much larger than she was. She said that her collateral material (brochure, stationery) gave her the look of being larger— "otherwise, we would not have received the contracts that we did."

Business Image—Learning From the Larger Companies

I often find myself saying to my clients, "You don't have to reinvent the wheel." There are some wonderful ideas and products out there. With a little tailor-made modification, they will work for your business. For example, a young businessman wanted to start his own business, and knew only that he wanted to get into manufacturing. By going to a trade show he found a cleaning product that was not doing well. He bought the license and patent, made some changes, and started manufacturing the product. In less than eighteen months, he was selling thousands of these nationally and is going international with his product within the year.

In contrast, sometimes you want to build on an already strong image. *Time* magazine recently redesigned its cover and copy. The famous red border is still there, but now there is a new, enlarged logo on the cover. Henry Muller, managing editor since 1987, said, "The priority was to define what a news magazine would be in the era of instant communications." He also says that "five years ago when we started to talk about this, two-thirds of the magazine was still driven by last week's news. Now, two-thirds of the magazine is original." As a result, it has been said to be more accessible and reader-friendly.

Summary

What is the image you are trying to portray to your clients and prospective customers? Research has shown that the closer you are to your clients or customers in attitudes, values, interests, and background, the more attractive they perceive you. Seven ways to sell yourself and your product or service include becoming knowledgeable in what you're selling, believing in what you are selling, showing how what you're selling will meet the needs and wants of the buyer, making what you say consistent with how you say it, dressing appropriately for what you are selling, being enthusiastic about what you are doing, and passionately believing that what you are selling will help the buyer in some way.

There are several inexpensive and time-saving ways to build your business image. They include developing a mission statement, writing personal and business biographies with important information, selecting a mascot or personal trademark, developing a firm and assertive handshake, dressing for impact, using good body language, initiating proper personal introductions, using good table manners, and developing a professional and consistent image through marketing tools such as slogans, stationery, brochures, and newsletters.

Notes

1. John T. Molloy, *The New Dress for Success* (New York: Warner Books, 1988).

14

When Customers Come Knocking on Your Door

There is a danger point for every small business when attracting customers is no longer the major problem. Often a business does not have the capital to finance an expansion, or existing employees can't handle the additional business, or a new marketing strategy is needed to make things work better. At this point, a small business is likely to make changes that erode the existing customer base.

The Critical Turning Points

Has the earlier success of your business begun to dwindle? Are you working more and making less? Consider the following indicators of a looming business crisis:

- You are spending over fifty hours a week at your job with no relief in sight.
- You answer your own phone at least 95 percent of the time.
- Your work intrudes upon your family, vacation time, or leisure more times than not.
- There's new equipment available that would save you time or money.
- You are marketing your business to the few 3 to 5 percent deadbeats rather than the 95 to 98 percent good customers.
- You can't separate your work from your ego.
- You run your business from a negative attitude rather than a positive one.

- You find yourself apologizing for your services or products.
- You can't find customer-service workable options.
- You change the rules several times in one day or week.
- You don't have time to market your business.
- You don't have time to do anything but work.
- You plan your lunch and dinner breaks around work every day.
- Your monthly income is healthy, but you don't have any cash at the end of the month.
- You spend the better half of each day putting out fires.
- You spend most of your day doing things that could easily be done by others.
- You have no clue as to how to increase your cash flow.
- You find yourself "floating" the majority of your checks each month.
- You don't have the time to do marketing, but you're looking for new business.

Analyze Your Situation

Expanding your business may well be a viable option for you and may solve some of your current operating problems. However, before considering expansion, look at your present operation to be sure it is as efficient and effective as it could be.

For example, I was approached by a landscaper in a moderate-size community who saw his cash-flow problems at best solved through an expansion of his services. I did not immediately agree, however. His landscaping and gardening business maintained over sixty-five gardens on a weekly basis and full landscaping jobs in between. The owner was nice and professional, but highly disorganized. He had two crews working five to six days a week—a busy business, but did not have the capital to finance an expansion. Mismanagement of time had cost him hundreds of thousands of dollars over the years. And in the last couple of years, he had not been able to save any money. In fact, he was close to bankruptcy.

I had the landscaper keep a time line for two weeks. He wrote down, in thirty-minute intervals, two weeks' worth of activities. Once we got a baseline, we knew where to begin a comprehensive time-management program. We were able to analyze where he was wasting time and how he could better spend most of his day. Ultimately he would expand his business, but the first step was getting his books in order.

Keep Your Present Customers

Before looking for new business, you want to make sure that your existing customers are happy. One of the biggest reasons customers change businesses or service providers is that they feel the business is no longer taking care of their needs, and they're tired of asking. A competitor comes along and grabs the customers away. And then, of course, there's the more dangerous situation when the customers don't say anything and just leave. I call them the "silent unsatisfied." A business doesn't know what's wrong until they are no longer customers, and the chance of getting them back is nil.

For my landscaper client, we prepared a customer-survey form asking them to jot down anything that needed attention by the crew. The survey was sent out with the monthly bill and looked like this:

Dear Client,

We want to continue to make you satisfied with our gardening services and happy with your garden. Please take a few extra minutes and tell us how we're doing and mail it back to us with your check. We would like to say thank you in advance by taking 10 percent off your next month's bill.

Client:_____   Month:_____

Clients _____

Groundcover   ☐

Grass   ☐

Weeds	☐
Flower Beds	☐
Lawn	☐
Fertilizer	☐
Grass	☐
Trees	☐
Plants	☐
Flowers	☐
Annuals	☐
Roses	☐
Edges	☐
Azaleas/Camellias/ Gardenias	☐
Too Dry	☐
Too Wet	☐
Clean-up	☐
Sprinklers	☐
Any other	☐

The results of the survey lowered the number of customers' calls "to get things taken care of" by 60 percent.

Another client, an accounting firm, was ready to expand but because of cash-flow problems was unable to do so. The business was there, but something internally was not working properly. While we were developing marketing strategies to bring in new business, we wanted to keep existing clients happy. We developed the following performance–customer service checkup:

Dear Customer (Customer's name),

We enjoy working with you and would appreciate it if you would take the time to answer these questions. It's our way of checking up on our performance and service to you. Please fill out the survey and mail it in the enclosed envelope. We would like to say "Thank You" in advance by taking $50 off your next invoice!

1. We deliver what we say we will punctually?   Yes   No
Explain_____.

2. Our prices are fair for the amount of work we do for you.
                                              Yes   No
Explain_____.

3. We produce results for you and your business.   Yes   No
Explain_____.

4. Our service is   FAIR   GOOD   EXCELLENT
Explain_____.

5. What can we do to help you further in your business?
Explain_____.

The results found the clients were frustrated with the accountants not returning their calls on a timely basis. Their service was rated fair. As one client who was surveyed said, "I pay my accountant later than I should, but he returns my calls later than *he* should."

The accounting firm hired an accounting service assistant to reroute calls to their proper destinations, provide more efficient client scheduling, and write a semi-annual newsletter on tax relief for their clients.

It's important to keep your survey short and to the point. Customers don't mind filling these out if they are brief and convenient to use. Keep your questions down to five or less.

Customers need an incentive for taking out valuable time to complete the survey. After all, in most cases they don't see it affecting their bottom line. A reduction on their next invoice greatly helps increase the number of responses.

Look for New Business

When you are ready, develop a plan to bring in more business. For the landscaper, we made a master plan of his sixty-plus customers, laid out on ten pages, with six customers per page. The client used blue ink for things he wanted to remember to do to their gardens—fertilize, weed—and red ink for things the customer wanted done.

We then took pictures of the gardens in different categories—middle-income residential properties, high-income residential properties, church gardens, and apartment landscaping. The landscaper then "worked the neighborhood," going to a minimum of twenty surrounding homes, churches, and apartment buildings, handing them pictures of similar-type gardens and introducing himself and his services. Results: Picked up 25 percent more new neighbor yards within four months than in the previous twelve months.

Additional Employees for Additional Business

Many small-business owners do all the work by themselves and slowly watch their volume grow. There comes a point, however, when they must move on to other ways of doing business. To do otherwise means a life of *only* hard work.

The printing business is one of great accuracy, timeliness, and professionalism. I was quite impressed initially with a local printer because he went that extra mile—he found two errors before my brochure went to press. (Of course, this is a case where proofing should be part of the service, but normally is not.) On the next job, however, I encountered a problem. My graphic artist had designed a brochure as a two-color job—gray and teal. The first problem arose when the printer could not print the black and white pictures clean and blamed the problem on the gray color. I asked the printer about options, since my client did not like the finished product, nor did I.

The client needed the brochure, and time was running out, so I had the printer rerun the brochure with black ink at an extra charge of $350. Then the printer did not have the brochures ready on time because of a broken piece of machinery. Then he would not release the finished 2,000 brochures until the invoice was paid. The situation got ugly but my responsibility was to my client, who by now was very frustrated. Eventually I got the brochures but had to pay for two print runs.

This particular printer—and many small businesses like it—are staffed only by the owner, who works six to seven days a week, often twelve hours a day, and occasionally is helped by a part-timer. The printer employed his dad part time, and he also answered his own phone, did the billing, and even occasionally delivered the work "if he got the chance." Here is a business owner who has hit the point of turning himself and his business into a liability.

The printer's failure to expand and hire qualified help not only cost him my business but the business of other professionals with whom I will share my bad experience. In fact, whenever the word *printer* comes up, I say "Stay away from this one."

In the long run, an owner needs to hire a full-time employee to answer phone calls, accept new jobs, follow up on existing jobs, and help in other ways. I make heavy use of printed materials in my business. The money I spend on printing each year would pay more than half that employee's salary. And I have learned that my bad experience is not an isolated one. It's similar to the drunk driver who is picked up on a DUI (drinking under the influence of alcohol). The chances are good that this person drinks and drives much more often than he is arrested.

Marketing Strategies to Make the Changes Work

Expanding your business puts a strain on existing operations. I cannot stress enough how important it is to keep your existing clients happy while you work at bringing in new ones. To begin, develop six different marketing strategies and guesstimate how much money each will take to implement. Then, take three at a time and work them. If one of the strategies is to hire one or two part-time employees, estimate the cost and work toward that goal.

Outsourcing

Small businesses should consider outsourcing. In other words, use a temporary agency for part-time secretarial, phone, filing, or other help during heavy loads. This is particularly beneficial in cyclical businesses, where people are extremely busy certain months of the year. Figure out what days or times each day you are the busiest.

With a temporary agency, you do not need to spend time interviewing candidates. If you don't like the person the agency sends, call for a replacement. You do not have to pay workers' compensation or payroll taxes. You do not have to write out a payroll, and you can use temps only when you need the help, rather than keep someone on your payroll as a burden to your cash flow. If you're a very small business and don't have the cash flow to expand or hire permanent help, use help only during the busiest four hours of your day.

If you have an advertising agency or a marketing business, outsource your graphic art. This works well for two main reasons: artists are in business for themselves and are more apt to keep on deadline; and by using several different artists, you get a greater variety of looks than usually come from a single firm.

You are probably better off hiring an answering service to handle your calls than depend on a machine. An answering service is far more professional than an answering machine. The basic cost of an answering service is between $35 and $50 a month, quite inexpensive compared to a full-time receptionist.

A Time-Management System

Create a time-management system that takes these ideas into consideration:

- Establish certain days of the week or times of the day to market for new clients. Mike, a safety professional, sets Wednesdays to meet with prospective clients. "I like the middle of the week to do prospect marketing. I make an effort to personally stop by clients I am working with," says Mike.
- Establish specific days of the week or times of the day to check your client list and see how things are going or how a product or service is working out. Kenyon Sills, owner of an advertising specialty company, says "I call a client usually in the afternoon, within a week after they receive the order to find out how the project or items worked. I stay right on top of things this way."

• Follow a master calendar that lists promised dates for projects or materials. A tip: always suggest a deadline seven days past the time you need. When developing brochures or newsletters, give yourself an extra three weeks. Any time a third or fourth party is involved (printer, artist), there are delays and you are ultimately responsible for the finished product. Save yourself a lot of stress and add three weeks at the beginning. Give your client a time frame and deliver early.

• Plan a minimum of thirty minutes to an hour to relax and get your mind off the business. Even though you may not be consciously thinking about business, your subconscious is working at solving a problem. Give yourself permission to relax and see the results that develop.

Mary Lou Romagno, author and motivational speaker, was looking for a title for her new seminar series. She says, "The harder I tried to think of a title, the more stumped I became. I decided to walk away from it for a weekend. The next day I came up with the title 'Prosperity for Success' while I was driving to the grocery store."

• Leave the building for lunch (although occasional desk lunches are unavoidable). If you eat your lunch at the office, walk around the block afterwards. Get out of the office! Every other week, I eat lunch at my desk and take a brisk walk two blocks away to buy a newspaper. Giving myself a destination helps get me out of the office.

• Spend a minimum of two hours a week reading articles in your field. Read articles and books that may solve problems or questions about cash-flow management, time management, marketing strategies, or promotional ideas. Use the information, modify it. That's why they were written—to be used!

I read for approximately thirty minutes before bed. The information I pull from a variety of sources gets used in my books, for developing client marketing strategies, and in seminars and speeches.

• Keep your clients updated on what's happening. Constant follow-up and communications are excellent marketing strategies. I have several clients that implemented this idea and they receive more business now than ever. An estate attorney keeps in touch with over 1,800 contacts via his quarterly newsletter. "I constantly receive calls from clients' referrals and am incredibly busy."

- If you haven't heard from a client or customer in the last month, give a call and say "Hi." I use four different temporary agencies, but received a call from one three weeks after my last work order. The owner called to say hello and two days later, guess which agency I called to do some telemarketing?

Summary

Expanding your business is risky and sometimes difficult. Financing the expansion and training new employees to handle the additional business become high priorities. Look for the critical turning points, such as when your monthly income is healthy, but you don't have any cash flow at the end of the month; when you are spending the better half of each day putting out fires; when you're spending most of your day on things that could easily be done by others without your expertise; when you find yourself "floating" the majority of your checks each month; and when you don't have the time to do marketing, but you're looking for new business anyway.

Create a time-management system that allows you to establish certain days of the week or times of the day to market for new clients, and other times to check on existing clients. Develop a large master calendar with dates for projects and deadlines, time to relax, and time to read articles and books. Keep your clients happy and new ones will come knocking on your door.

15

Stress Reducers for Creative Marketing

Over the years I have found that the best way to stay creative is to keep the stress down. I devote this entire chapter to ways of keeping the everyday frustrations, deadlines, anxieties, and challenges in check while keeping the door to creative marketing open. According to the Mitchum Report on Stress in the 1990s, conducted by Research and Forecasts, Inc., "most Americans say they experience 'some to a lot' of stress in their daily lives."

We all need a certain amount of stress to be productive. However, problems arise when our body's "fight or flight" reaction continues over a long period of time. The physiological response to a negative stressor is no different from that to a positive stressor. In either event, a person needs to learn to relax. The elation from being newly married or developing a new business is energy draining, as are the stresses that comes with cash-flow problems.

"Stress can be fantastic or fatal," says Dr. Peter G. Hanso, author of *The Joy of Stress*. "The most electrifying performances occur before a live audience—not during rehearsal. Too much stress, however, can be counterproductive. After three weeks of being nit-picked by a lunatic director, even the best actor might not perform up to par."[1]

We've all been in situations where we are extremely tense and have a difficult time remembering something, whereas in a normal state of mind it would be easy to recall. Physiologically, our creative minds shut down under stress. Muscles tighten, more blood is pumped through the veins, and the body gets ready to protect itself. According to Susan Seliger, author of *Stop Killing Yourself*, chronic stress takes a toll on your health. "Tensed muscles, when there is no pouncing or running to do, result in headaches, back-aches and insomnia. Over time, elevated heartbeat leads to high blood pressure. And the stress hormones, if not burned up in a burst of flight, build up in the blood to damage vessels and clog arteries, leading to heart disease or heart attacks."[2]

Research shows that stress lowers the entire immune system, allowing diseases to infiltrate the body easily. A client of mine recently had bronchitis. She went back to work early, and came down with pneumonia. Some days, she felt so bad that she had to go home and rest. I often wonder if she could have saved herself anxiety, pain, and time away from her business if she had taken the full recovery time after her original diagnosis.

The Stress Reducers

Let's look at some ways to keep your stress down and your creative juices flowing.

Exercise

Almost any type of exercise (swimming, walking, bicycling, running, jumping rope) helps to keep stress at bay. Consistency is the key here. Most experts agree that exercise three to four times a week, for a minimum of twenty minutes, is best. Consistent exercise tends to keep blood pressure and heart rate low. Research has shown that exercise releases endorphins, a morphinelike substance that minimizes pain and gives an all-around good feeling. If you're physically fit, the endorphin released in your body gives a boost known as "runner's high." This boost allows you to push yourself harder.

TIME TIP: *Stay conscious of exercise opportunities as you go through your day. For example, use the stairs rather than the elevator. As you walk down the hall to pick up mail, receive a client, or go to the rest room, swing your arms, twist your waist, and hold in your stomach. Walk to lunch. If you eat at your desk, walk around the block, taking in deep breaths and slowly letting them out as you stretch.*

Meditate

There are many different ways to meditate and get positive results. The one thing that rings true for me is to completely relax and not allow worries into my conscious thinking. This gives the body and mind time to relax and allows the subconscious to relax as well. A computer analyst, Mary Samuels, has recently taken up meditation and yoga. "It feels wonderful. I'm relaxed after a session and also feel energized," she says.

TIME TIP: One of the best times to meditate is early in the morning. It is a great way to start the day with energy and focus. Another good time is after lunch. Turn the lights off, listen to music, sit in one chair and put your legs up in another, hold all calls, shut your eyes, and meditate for ten to fifteen minutes. It helps you to focus and maintain a feeling of "calm" for the afternoon.

Stretch and Breathe

My three children, ages 12 to 17, started taking karate three months ago. They opted to go five days a week, even though I had signed them up for only four. One of the things they enjoy most about karate is the stretching! I grew up in dance shoes and never liked the stretching.

TIME TIP: Jane Tiptor, a computer troubleshooter, says "I'll stretch at my desk while I'm writing, and breathe in and slowly breathe out. It works wonders on my lower back and shoulders. In addition, I intermittently stand up and slowly and deliberately swing my arms from one side to another, taking a deep breath and slowly letting it out. This works with head rotations as well."

Change Your Perception of Stress

What is stressful for me is not necessarily what you would find stressful. Stress is in the eyes of the beholder. We only have to look as far as another family member to see the differences in perceptions of stress. I may get stressed over something at work and my husband cannot understand what made it so stressful. My younger niece would cry if she spilled juice. She now looks around to get the "cue" if she should cry or simply say "I'm sorry."

Leo F. Buscaglia, author and speaker, says, "The quality of your life can be improved tremendously if you view it in a different perspective."[3]

TIME TIP: Use the "What is the worst thing that could happen" approach when you get into a stressful situation. Realize the worst-case scenario and then work back. In most instances, it is not a situation of life or death. Monitoring your stress helps change your perceptions to more realistic ones. Think of solutions to problems rather than the hopelessness of them.

Eat a Balanced Diet

What you eat directly affects your body. A balanced diet helps maintain your energy as well as give you a positive mental framework. Fresh vegetables and fruits boost energy, provide essential vitamins, contain necessary water, and satisfy a sweet tooth.

TIME TIP: Keep cut-up vegetables (you can buy them already cut) in the refrigerator on a plate for easy access. Cut up a variety of fruit while you're making dinner or breakfast, and keep it in the refrigerator, also on a plate for a quick pick-me-up. Put vegetables and fruit in separate baggies and take them to work. If you forget to take the vegetables and fruit to the office, stop off at a grocery store.

Actively Face the Stress

Stress comes from anticipated fear of what *may* happen and rarely does. Tax audits can do this to you, cross words will make you feel stressful, saying yes too many times will activate your stress.

Taking control of your life is an excellent way to actively face the stress. Think of your options and seek solutions. Your subconscious has wonderful powers; given the chance, it will help you come up with solutions. Start thinking about your options and write them down. If a solution is not in sight, that's okay. Give your subconscious time to think about the possibilities as you go about your life. Chances are very good that, in time, your subconscious will solve the problem. However, it is important to keep the stress down, or physiologically your mind will not operate at its creative best.

TIME TIP: *Think of the problem you need to resolve, then let it go and think about something else. Exercise, meditate, or get involved in a new activity. Let your inner computer do the rest.*

Write It Down

Why congest the mind more than necessary? You get literally thousands of stimuli competing for your attention. It's much easier to remember and keep ideas organized if they're written down. Several of my clients find it hard to fall asleep at night because they think about the day's events or what they're planning for the next day. It's a good idea to rehash the day's events so that you can move on in a positive direction, or to plan the following day. But it's far more effective to do these things on paper. You'll remember your ideas and clear your mind at the same time.

TIME TIP: *Keep a pad nearby during the day and one at your nightstand with a pen beside it, just in case you need to write something down, whether it be an idea, a problem, a solution, or someone to call in the morning. Writing things down clears your mind, making it easier for you to fall asleep. Susan Dags, owner of a billing company, says "I started writing down my thoughts before bed and finally was able to sleep through the night."*

Visualize Success

The concept of *visualization*—visualizing yourself making a sales goal, sales pitch, or any other type of behavior or feeling—is popular today. "Seeing it in your mind's eye" gives you a chance to rehearse what you want to say, do, or feel before the real thing happens.

Patients have visualized themselves healthy, slimmer, and happier. This rehearsal gets you familiar with positive outcomes.

If you are planning to give a speech, visualize yourself giving the speech, visualize what your hands are doing and how confident you're feeling, visualize how easily the words come and how you confidently handle questions and answers. If you want to lose weight, visualize yourself as your slim ideal—how you look in clothes, how you feel pounds lighter, how you act—and visualize your inner feelings about yourself.

TIME TIP: During your quiet fifteen to twenty minutes each day, visualize yourself healthy, slim, confident, or anything else you would like to achieve. It's good for your mind and your body.

Keep a Thank-You File

There are times when you have to spend time so that you can save time. Writing thank-you notes takes time, but in the long run it nourishes relationships and saves you time. For example, I sent a press release with a note to a staff writer at our local newspaper. She came to cover the fund-raiser on Saturday and went on and on about how she loved the note I sent her *over a year ago.* I would venture to say that we will receive good press for this last event, too.

TIME TIP: Keep one sheet of a legal pad for listing thank-you's you need to write. For example, last Saturday I had a book signing in the afternoon and a fund-raiser at our house that evening. I had over sixteen thank-you's to write for these two events.

Read

How do you keep the business running and have time to read? There are some business people who, despite the many other demands on their time, make time to read. Reading helps to solve problems, is an avenue for generating motivation, and is a resource for information. Regis McKenna, author of *The Regis Touch,* says "To deal with today's world as a businessman you have to be able to think, and you want literature that stimulates you to think. You don't want prescriptive answers—they don't apply."[4]

TIME TIP: *Reading, making copies of pages or articles, and filing them saves you time when you need to retrieve this invaluable information for speeches, seminars, and presentations.*

Stay in Control of Your Time

There are only twenty-four hours in a day. Take away sleep time, and that leaves approximately sixteen to seventeen hours. In order to take control of your time, you need to review your calendar several times a day. If you're falling behind because a project is taking longer than anticipated, or you are waiting for clients, there are a few things you can do:

- Reschedule an appointment later in the day. Most people will welcome the additional time to do their work and happily reschedule the appointment.
- Hold calls. Hold your calls for thirty or forty-five minutes, or an hour to "catch up" on the work.
- Take ten. Force yourself to take ten minutes to shut your eyes, relax, and get re-focused again.

Here are a few other ways to take control of your time.

- *Just say no.* Remember that you are not doing anyone justice by overcommitting yourself. Give a simple, "I appreciate you thinking of me, but I'm unable to say yes at this time." You do not need to offer any explanation.
- *Set your priorities.* What do you need to accomplish today? Write down your "To Do" list. Then choose two things that, if you did them, you would feel as though you accomplished a lot. Staying focused by doing two top-priority activities will increase your productivity and lower your stress. When you've accomplished those two priorities, then choose two more for the day. You will be surprised how focused you remain.
- *Let negative feelings go.* You basically have two choices in any situation: you can change the situation or you can accept the situation. In either case, let the negative feelings go. Ask yourself, "If I stay negative, will it help the situation?" If the answer is no, then let the negativity go. Negative feelings only bring stress and anxi-

ety—two feelings that stifle creativity and productivity. Is it really worth staying negative?

TIME TIP: Keep a month-at-a-glance calendar only. It's much easier to keep control of your time and life when you can see it a month at a glance. It helps to keep deadlines, busy appointment days, and concentrated work times in constant view. No surprises when you turn the page.

Ten Proverbs to Lessen Your Time Stress

1. To avoid guilt is to balance, not juggle, your time and your life. Balancing your life leads to less stress than juggling.
2. To develop alternate plans is to gain self-esteem. It's important to plan for alternate plan B and C and D if your first choice doesn't work.
3. To find the time for love is to feel and nurture the real you and accept your vulnerabilities. If you don't have time to nurture yourself, or think it's a waste of time, then your life is probably full of stress.
4. To take control of your schedule is to take responsibility for your life. You're the one who writes down your appointments and you're the one who can make the necessary changes.
5. To spend time to save time is to recognize your own value. There are times when you need to take the initial time to save time later.
6. To make decisions, right or wrong, is to exercise your freedom. Only if you make decisions do you have the freedom to be yourself.
7. To control the telephone is to accept it as your business associate. The telephone is your partner in business if you don't let it control your time. Have a secretary or machine screen your calls, and return calls at designated times.
8. To delegate is to trust in your ability to let go of control. Giving others the opportunity to make decisions develops internal strength.
9. To use waiting time is to enjoy the process on the way to your goals. Use waiting time to take a deep breath, to reflect on an issue, to read a magazine, or to sit and do nothing.

10. To make a commitment is to focus your sights and expend your energy on personal priorities. Setting personal and work priorities keeps you focused and makes it easier to say yes or no to overload.

Summary

A certain amount of stress is productive. But an overabundance of stress lowers the immune system, opening the body to disease. Eleven ways to keep stress under control are through a regular exercise program, meditation, stretches and breathing techniques, changes in your perception of stress, a balanced diet, facing a stress situation, writing down your fears, visualizing success, keeping a thank-you file, reading to solve problems and create new projects, and staying in control of your time.

Notes

1. Peter Hanson, *The Joy of Stress* (Kansas City: Andrews, McMeel & Parker, 1986).
2. Susan Seliger, *Stop Killing Yourself: Make Stress Work for You* (New York: Putnam, 1984).
3. Leo Buscaglia, "Happiness—Put Joy Back Into Your Life," *Complete Woman*, April 1990.
4. Regis McKenna, *The Regis Touch: Million-Dollar Advice From America's Top Marketing Consultant* (Reading, Mass.: Addison-Wesley, 1985).

16

Beyond the Time-Marketing Equation

As we have discussed in this book, the Time-Marketing Equation runs through every business. In other words, your *method* of bringing products and services to your customers is paramount.

Your customers and clients will buy what you are selling if they *perceive* your product or service to benefit them. "It's not how you wrap your product, it's how they receive your wrap. It's not how you package your service, it's how they perceive that service," says William R. 'Max' Carey, Jr., founder and chief executive of Corporate Resource Development, Inc., in Atlanta.

Mind positioning is different from product or service positioning. A great deal of expensive advertising focuses on product or service positioning, whereas mind positioning depends on understanding motivation and targeting emotions.

Taking a motivational approach to marketing can appreciably reduce the time required to close a sale and develop a loyal customer base. A *motive* is something that causes motion, that prompts, that incites to action, that determines the choice or moves the will. Any time you are influencing another person, you are motivating.

The goal in the Time-Marketing Equation is for customers to believe your product or service is the best for them and their situation; for customers to filter through their perceptions what will work and move them to buy. Behavior is complex. What motivates one person to buy may demotivate another. In other words, your customers may behave in similar ways for different reasons, or different motives. Customers buy because of expected results:

Behavior	Expected Results
Start a business	More independence
	Makes me look important
	Makes me look successful
	More control of my schedule
Advertising	Outspend my competition
	Name recognition
	Loss leader, just get the customer in the door
Work 60+ hours a week	Loves the job
	Too much to do
	Enjoys work more than home
	Wants a partnership
Target customers ages 20–40	Wants to stay young and "with it"
	Can identify with this age group
	Wants a slice of their expendable income

Motivation is an important concept for employees, vendors, and customers. It is the driving force behind communications, sales, and marketing. How do you use this human behavior to everyone's advantage? Read the signals provided by your customers, individually and generally.

Individual Signals

Just as clients will tell you how to make your products or services better and more customer-friendly, so too they will tell you who they are and what motivates them.

Some signals your customer shares with you are the *type* of car they drive, the type of clothes they wear, the type of watch they wear, the type of hobbies they're interested in, the way they spend their leisure time and money, the pictures they have on their office wall or desk—and, of course, what they like to talk about.

Develop a creative market-driven plan that includes convenience and time-saving strategies for your customers. "The watchword for the streamlined 1990s will be multifunction," says Faith Popcorn. "Products that accomplish two or three things at once, or that allow you to get more than one job done at a time."[1]

Remember: Ideas are only as good as their implementation!

Note

1. Faith Popcorn, *The Popcorn Report* (New York: Bantam Doubleday Dell, 1991). Copyright © 1991 by Faith Popcorn. Used by permission of Doubleday, a division of Bantam Doubleday Dell Publishing Group, Inc.

Index